My Bedtime Bible

Published by World Bible Publishers, Inc., Iowa Falls, IA 50126

ISBN 0-529-10248-X

Printed in the United States of America

2 3 4 5 6 — 99 98 97 96 95

My Bedtime Bible

Carolyn Larsen

Illustrated by **Rick Incrocci**

WORLD PUBLISHING

GRAND RAPIDS, MICHIGAN 49418 U.S.A.

Contents

Week Five — God Wants Us to Obey Him
    Sunday – Obedience Saves Noah   Genesis 6:9-22
    Monday – Abraham Obeys   Genesis 22:1-19
    Tuesday – Trust and Obey   Numbers 14:26-35; Deuteronomy 1:8-46
    Wednesday – Moses Loses His Temper   Numbers 20:6-12;
                                      Deuteronomy 3:21-29.
    Thursday – Rahab's Reward   Joshua 2; 6:22-23
    Friday – Jonah Obeys   Jonah
    Saturday – Jamie Disobeys

Week Six — God Is Our Protector
    Sunday – Lot Is Saved   Genesis 19:4-16
    Monday – Baby Moses Is Saved   Exodus 2:1-10
    Tuesday – The Passover   Exodus 12:1-30
    Wednesday – Esther   Esther
    Thursday – The Fiery Furnace   Daniel 3
    Friday – Hungry Lions   Daniel 6
    Saturday – Ice Cream Danger

Week Seven — God Says How to Live
    Sunday – Only One God   Exodus 20:3
    Monday – Be Careful What You Say   Exodus 20:7
    Tuesday – God Wants Us to Go to Church   Exodus 20:8-11
    Wednesday – Respect Your Father and Mother   Exodus 20:12
    Thursday – Be Careful How You Treat Others   Exodus 20:13-16
    Friday – Wanting What Someone Else Has   Exodus 20:17
    Saturday – Sunday Morning Blues

Week Eight — God Has a Plan
    Sunday – Bad Dreams, Good Dreams   Genesis 37, 40–41
    Monday – Joseph Saves His Family   Genesis 42, 45
    Tuesday – Ruth and Naomi   Ruth
    Wednesday – Nehemiah's Sadness   Nehemiah 2
    Thursday – Daniel and the King's Dream   Daniel 2
    Friday – David Is Chosen   1 Samuel 16:1-13
    Saturday – Game Plans

Week Nine — God Gives Us Families

Sunday – The First Babies	Genesis 4:1-2
Monday – The Miracle Baby	Genesis 21:1-7
Tuesday – A Bride for Isaac	Genesis 24
Wednesday – Fighting Brothers	Genesis 25:19-26
Thursday – Big Sister Babysits	Exodus 2:4, 7
Friday – Long Awaited Child	1 Samuel 1
Saturday – Family Reunion	

Week Ten — God Gives Strength

Sunday – Crossing the Jordan	Joshua 3
Monday – Deborah and Barak	Judges 4:6-15
Tuesday – Gideon's Little Army	Judges 7:1-22
Wednesday – Ruth Leaves Home	Ruth 1:16-17
Thursday – David Spares Saul's Life	1 Samuel 24
Friday – David Becomes King	2 Samuel 5:1-5
Saturday – I'm Scared	

Week Eleven — God Is Always with You

Sunday – God Remembers Noah	Genesis 8
Monday – Jacob's Dream	Genesis 28:10-22
Tuesday – Joseph	Genesis 39:20-23
Wednesday – Clouds and Fire	Exodus 13:21-22
Thursday – Thirsty People	Exodus 15:22-25
Friday – A New Leader	Joshua 1:1-5
Saturday – The Dark Room	

Week Twelve — God Is Love

Sunday – Best Friends	1 Samuel 20
Monday – Loving Your Enemies	2 Samuel 9
Tuesday – Elijah's Reward	2 Kings 2:1-11
Wednesday – Help for a Widow	2 Kings 4:1-7
Thursday – Showing Love to God	1 Chronicles 22:6-7; 2 Chronicles 2–3
Friday– Unexpected Love	Ezra 1:5-11
Saturday – Jamie Shows Love	

Week Thirteen — God Gives Wisdom

Sunday – God Helps Joseph	Genesis 41:1–39

Tuesday – God Loved the World	John 3:16
Wednesday – Believe	John 14:6
Thursday – Confess	1 John 1:9
Friday – Repent	Acts 3:19
Saturday – Jamie's Decision	

Week Eighteen — Psalms about Good versus Bad
    Sunday – Psalm 1
    Monday – Psalm 36
    Tuesday – Psalm 37
    Wednesday – Psalm 73
    Thursday – Psalm 112
    Friday – Psalm 119:1-8, 89-96
    Saturday – Jamie's Memory Verse

Week Nineteen — Thank You Psalms
    Sunday – Psalm 18
    Monday – Psalm 33
    Tuesday – Psalm 66
    Wednesday – Psalm 107
    Thursday – Psalm 118
    Friday – Psalm 139
    Saturday – Jamie Says "Thank You"

Week Twenty — Proverbs To Live By

Sunday – Choose Good Friends	Proverbs 1:8-19
Monday – Trust	Proverbs 3:5-6
Tuesday – Right vs. Wrong	Proverbs 4:10-27
Wednesday – Don't Be Lazy	Proverbs 6:6-11
Thursday – Mom and Dad's Love	Proverbs 13:24; 22:6
Friday – Listen to Wisdom	Proverbs 8:12-36
Saturday – Jamie's Job	

Week Twenty-One — More Proverbs To Live By

Sunday – Be Careful What You Say	Proverbs 11:12-13
Monday – True Happiness	Proverbs 15:16; 16:8
Tuesday – Constructive Criticism	Proverbs 15:31-33

Thursday – Love Your Enemies · · · · · · · · · · · Matthew 5:43-48
Friday – Be Generous · · · · · · · · · · · · · · · · · · Matthew 6:1-4
Saturday – Jamie's Offering

Week Twenty-Six — More Sermon on the Mount
Sunday – Do Not Worry · · · · · · · · · · · · · Matthew 6:25-34
Monday – Do Not Judge Others · · · · · · · · · Matthew 7:1-6
Tuesday – Ask, Seek, Knock · · · · · · · · · · · Matthew 7:7-12
Wednesday – Narrow Gate · · · · · · · · · · · · Matthew 7:13-14
Thursday – Be Fruitful · · · · · · · · · · · · · · Matthew 7:15-23
Friday – The Foolish Builder · · · · · · · · · · Matthew 7:24-29
Saturday – Answer for Yourself

Week Twenty-Seven — The Miracles of Jesus
Sunday – The Miracle Water · · · · · · · · · · · · · · · John 2:1-11
Monday – The Quiet Storm   Matt. 8:23-27; Mark 4:35-41; Luke 8:22-25
Tuesday – Lunch for 5,000   Matt. 14:15-21; Mark 6:35-44; Luke 9:12-17
Wednesday – Walking on Water   Matt. 14:22-27; Mark 6:47-51;
John 6:16-21
Thursday – Fishing with Jesus · · · · · · · · · · · · · · Luke 5:4-11
Friday – Lazarus Is Alive · · · · · · · · · · · · · · · · John 11:1-44
Saturday – Jamie Is Afraid

Week Twenty-Eight — More Miracles of Jesus
Sunday – Blind Bartimaeus · · · · · · · · · · · · · Mark 10:46-52
Monday – The Deaf Mute · · · · · · · · · · · · · · · Mark 7:31-37
Tuesday – Jesus Heals a Woman with Great Faith · · Matt. 9:20-22;
Mark 5:25-29; Luke 8:43-48
Wednesday – Ten Lepers · · · · · · · · · · · · · · · · Luke 17:11-19
Thursday – Jairus' Daughter · · · · · · · · · · · · · Matt. 9:23-25;
Mark 5:22-42; Luke 8:41-56
Friday – A Healed Servant · · · · · · · Matt. 8:5-13; Luke 7:1-10
Saturday – Jamie Wants a Miracle

Week Twenty-Nine — Stories Jesus Told
Sunday – The Sower   Matthew13:1-23; Mark 4:3-20; Luke 8:5-16
Monday – Story of the Weeds · · · · · · · Matthew 13:24-30, 36-43
Tuesday –The Mustard Seed · · · · · Matthew 13:31-32; Mark 4:30-32;

Wednesday – Use Good Sense   Ephesians 5:15-20
Thursday – Children Obey Parents   Ephesians 6:1-3
Friday – The Armor of God   Ephesians 6:10-25
Saturday – Jamie Is Angry

Week Thirty-Four —The Last Days of Jesus

Sunday – Predicting His Death   Matthew 16:21-29;
Mark 8:31–9:1; Luke 9:22-27

Monday – Triumphal Entry   Matthew 21:1-11; Mark 11:1-10;
Luke 19:28-38; John 12:12-15

Tuesday – The Betrayal   Matthew 26:14-16; Mark 14:10-11; Luke 22:3-6

Wednesday – The Last Supper   Matthew 26:17-30;
Mark 14:12-26; Luke 22:7-22

Thursday – Crucify Him!   Matthew 27:11-56; Mark 15:2-41;
Luke 23:2-49

Friday – Jesus Is Buried   Matthew 27:57-61; Mark 15:42-47;
Luke 23:50-56; John 19:38-42

Saturday – Jamie Asks, "Why?"

Week Thirty-Five — He Is Alive!

Sunday – The Empty Tomb   Matthew 28:1-8; Mark 16:1-8;
Luke 24:1-10; John 20:1-9

Monday – Mary Sees Jesus   John 20:10-18
Tuesday – The Road to Emmaus   Luke 24:13-35
Wednesday – Doubting Thomas   John 20:24-29
Thursday – Breakfast with Friends   John 21:4-14
Friday – The Ascension   Luke 24:50-53; Acts 1:1-11
Saturday – Happy Easter!

Week Thirty-Six — Serving the Lord

Sunday – Dorcas   Acts 9:36-42
Monday – Serving God by Serving Others   Matthew 25:31-40
Tuesday – The Woman Who Gave Everything   Mark 12:41-44
Wednesday – Philip Obeys   Acts 8:26-39
Thursday – Stephen   Acts 6
Friday – A Second Chance   Acts 15:36-41; Colossians 4:10-11;
2 Timothy 4:11

Saturday – Jamie Serves God

Week Thirty-Seven –The First Church
    Sunday – A Special Gift   Acts 2:1-12
    Monday – Doing God's Work   Acts 3:1-10
    Tuesday – Overcoming Trouble   Acts 5:17-42
    Wednesday – Sharing with One Another   Acts 2:42-47; 4:32-37
    Thursday – Miracles   Acts 5:12-16
    Friday – Sending out Missionaries   Acts 13:1-5
    Saturday – My Church

Week Thirty-Eight – What Is Love?
    Sunday – Love Is Kind & Patient   1 Corinthians 13:4
    Monday – Love Is Not Rude or Selfish   1 Corinthians 13:5
    Tuesday – No Anger or Grudges   1 Corinthians 13:5
    Wednesday – Rejoices in Truth   1 Corinthians 13:6
    Thursday – Love Protects   1 Corinthians 13:7
    Friday – Love Never Fails   1 Corinthians 13:8
    Saturday – Jamie Shows Love

Week Thirty-Nine – Living for Christ
    Sunday – Deny Yourself   Luke 9:23
    Monday – Reading the Bible   John 8:31-32; 2 John 9
    Tuesday – Prayer   Matthew 7:7; John 14:13-14, 15:7
    Wednesday – Loving Others   John 13:34-35; 1 John 4:11-21
    Thursday – Bearing Fruit   John 15:5, 8, 16
    Friday – Working Together   1 Corinthians 12:12-31
    Saturday – When I Grow Up

Week Forty – Angels: God's Messengers
    Sunday – Abraham's Special Message   Genesis 18:1-15
    Monday – Lot Is Saved   Genesis 19:1-3, 15-25
    Tuesday – Balaam's Donkey   Numbers 22:21-35
    Wednesday – Baby Announcement   Judges 13:2-25
    Thursday – Food for Elijah   1 Kings 19:3-9
    Friday – Daniel and the Lions   Daniel 6
    Saturday – Jamie's Angel

Week Forty-One — More Angel Stories

Sunday – A Very Hot Furnace . . . . Daniel 3:1-30
Monday – An Announcement to Mary . . . . Luke 1:26-38
Tuesday – Announcement to the Shepherds . . . . Luke 2:8-14
Wednesday – Angels in Joseph's Dream . . . . . . Matthew 1:20; 2:13, 19
Thursday – Peter and John in Prison . . . . Acts 5:17-20
Friday – Peter in Prison . . . . Acts 12:1-11
Saturday – The Announcement

Week Forty-Two — Prayer

Sunday – The Way Not to Pray . . . . Matthew 6:5-8
Monday – The Lord's Prayer . . . . Matthew 6:9-13
Tuesday – Praise God! . . . . Ephesians 1:13-15; Hebrews 13:15
Wednesday – Giving Thanks! . . . . Mark 6:41; Romans 7:25;
Ephesians 5:4; Philippians 1:3
Thursday – Confession Is Good for the Soul . . . Luke 15:21; 1 John 1:9
Friday – Asking for What You Want . . . . Matthew 7:7-8;
Philippians 4:6; James 1:5-8
Saturday – "Now I Lay Me . . ."

Week Forty-Three — Sharing the Good News

Sunday – The Example of Paul . . . . Acts 18
Monday – Barnabas . . . . Acts 4:36-37; 11:22-26
Tuesday –Priscilla and Aquila . . . . Acts 18:24-28; Romans 16:3-5
Wednesday – Timothy . . . . 1 Corinthians 4:17; 1 Timothy 4:11-12;
2 Timothy 1:5
Thursday – Peter . . . . Acts 2:14-21
Friday – Silas . . . . Acts 16:16-34; 1 Peter 5:12
Saturday – Jamie Shares the Good News

Week Forty-Four — Learning God's Word

Sunday – Hearing the Word . . . . Luke 11:28; Romans 10:17; 1 Peter 2:2-3
Monday – Study God's Word . . . . Acts 17:11; Revelation 1:3
Tuesday – Memorize God's Word . . . . Psalm 119:9, 11
Wednesday – Think about God's Word . . . . Psalm 1:2-3; Philippians 4:8-9
Thursday – Living out God's Word . . . . James 1:22; 2:14-20
Friday – Sharing God's Word . . . . Matthew 28:19-20

Saturday – Jamie Learns God's Word

Week Forty-Five — The Fruit of the Spirit
    Sunday – The Gift of the Holy Spirit   Matthew 7:16-20; Galatians 5:16
    Monday – Love and Joy   Galatians 5:22
    Tuesday – Peace and Patience   Galatians 5:22
    Wednesday – Kindness and Goodness   Galatians 5:22
    Thursday – Faithfulness   Galatians 5:22
    Friday – Gentleness and Self-Control   Galatians 5:23
    Saturday – Jamie Learns about Growth

Week Forty-Six — Paul
    Sunday – Paul's First Time Preaching   Acts 9:19-31
    Monday – To Lystra   Acts 14:8-18
    Tuesday – Lydia's Conversion   Acts 16:11-15
    Wednesday –Paul Teaches in Athens   Acts 17:16-34
    Thursday – Eutychus   Acts 20:7-12
    Friday – Timothy   2 Timothy 3:10–4:8
    Saturday – Jamie's Hero

Week Forty-Seven — Old Testament Leaders
    Sunday – Noah Served When Others Didn't   Genesis 6–8
    Monday – Joash's Good Idea   2 Kings 11:21–12:16
    Tuesday – Joshua Obeys   Numbers 27:18-23; Joshua 1; 6
    Wednesday – Esther Is Not Afraid   Esther 2; 4–5
    Thursday – David Does Right   1 Samuel 17; 19; 26
    Friday – Moses Serves God   Exodus 3
    Saturday – Jamie Understands

Week Forty-Eight — New Testament Leaders
    Sunday – John the Baptist Prepares the way   Luke 3:1-23
    Monday – Peter Learns a Lesson   Acts 10
    Tuesday – Paul Keeps on Serving   Acts 21:1-14
    Wednesday – Jesus Chooses His family   Luke 6:12-16
    Thursday – John, Jesus' Friend   Matthew 17:1; John 13:23; 19:26;
          Revelation 1:9
    Friday – Timothy, the Young Preacher   1 Timothy 4:11; 2 Timothy
    Saturday – Jamie's Favorite

Week Forty-Nine — Children in the Bible

Sunday – Samuel Hears Voices .... 1 Samuel 3
Monday – A Slave Girl .... 2 Kings 5:1-14
Tuesday – Josiah .... 2 Kings 22:1–23:3
Wednesday – Children Who Wanted to See Jesus .... Luke 18:15-17
Thursday – The Boy with a Lunch .... John 6:1-15
Friday – Paul's Nephew .... Acts 23:12-22
Saturday – How Can I Serve?

Week Fifty — Getting Along with Others

Sunday – Love Each Other .... 1 John 3:18; 4:7-8
Monday – Encouraging Each Other .... Romans 12:18; 14:19; 15:2;
                                                                      Ephesians 4:12
Tuesday – Working Together .... Ecclesiastes 4:9-10; 1 Corinthians 9:19-23
Wednesday – Forgive Each Other .... Matthew 18:21-22; Ephesians 4:32
Thursday – Keep Meeting Together .... Acts 2:42; Hebrews 10:25
Friday – Be Unified .... Jeremiah 32:39; John 17:21; Acts 2:42
Saturday – Jamie Is Encouraged

Week Fifty-One — The Book of James

Sunday – True Religion Does Not Come Easy .... James 1:2-15
Monday – Faith Starts Everything .... James 1:16-27
Tuesday – Live Your Faith .... James 2:1–26
Wednesday – Wisdom Comes from God .... James 3:1-18
Thursday – Demonstrate Your Faith .... James 4:1-17
Friday – Show Your Faith by Prayer .... James 5:13-20
Saturday – Jamie's Faith

Week Fifty-Two — The Future

Sunday – Jesus Is Coming .... Luke 17:29-36
Monday – Judgment .... 1 Corinthians 3:12-15, 4:5
Tuesday – Believer's Hope ... Romans 8:38-39; Colossians 1:5; 1 John 2:28
Wednesday – Signs of His Return .... Matthew 24:3-14
Thursday – Heavenly Treasures .... Matthew 6:19-24
Friday – Praising God Forever .... Revelation 7:12; 19
Saturday – Hurry Up!

God Gives Good Gifts

Sunday

God Made the World

GENESIS 1:1-10

Do you like to play outside? What do you play? Do you build towns in a sandbox or ride a scooter? Do you like to look at fluffy clouds floating by?

Long ago there was no earth, no grass, not even any sunshine. Everything was dark and empty. But then God decided to make the world. He just said the words and there was the earth and sky. There was the sun and moon and stars. There was dry land and oceans. God made them all, just by saying the words.

The next time you play outside, remember to say, "Thank you" to God for giving us our world.

What is your favorite part of God's world?
Can you go out and look at the stars right now?

Dear God,
Your world is so big and full of things. I like the bright sunshine. It makes me feel warm and happy. I like the moon and twinkling stars. Thank you for making the world. Amen.

In the beginning, God created heaven and earth. GENESIS 1:1

God Made Plants and Trees

GENESIS 1:11-13

Do you like to eat crunchy apples or juicy oranges? Do you like to smell pretty flowers? What is your favorite kind of flower? Pink flowers, yellow flowers, big flowers, or little flowers?

Do you know where flowers and fruits come from? God made them. After he made the world, God filled it with all kinds of grasses, flowers, and trees. Some trees have fruit with seeds inside. That way more trees can grow from the seeds. Wasn't that a wonderful idea?

Look for the brown seeds inside an apple.

Can you plant seeds and watch for flowers to grow?

Dear God,
Thank you for flowers and for trees. Thank you for thinking of putting seeds in them so more flowers and trees will grow. Amen.

Everything came into existence through him. Not one thing that exists was made without him.

JOHN 1:3

19

God Filled the Oceans and Skies with Life

GENESIS 1:20-23

God has a wonderful imagination. He filled the oceans with tiny sea horses, eels that glow like lights, huge killer whales, and gentle dolphins.

God made songbirds that sing pretty songs. He made big bald eagles and tiny humming birds.

God was happy with all the fish and birds he made. He told them to have babies so there would always be fish in the seas and birds in the sky.

How many kinds of birds can you see in your back yard?

What is your favorite ocean animal?

Dear God,
You thought of so many wonderful kinds of sea creatures and birds. Thank you for little goldfish and the octopus with many legs. Thank you for pretty songbirds and honking geese. Amen.

The deeds of the LORD are spectacular. PSALM 111:2

God Made the First Man

GENESIS 1:24-31

Do you have a job to do such as cleaning your room or feeding the dog?

God made a beautiful world. Now he needed someone to take care of it. So God made the very first man. He named him Adam.

Adam was made to be like God. That means he could think and feel.

Adam's first job was to name all the animals that God had made. God marched them by Adam and he decided what to call them.

Do you have a pet that you helped name?
What name would you choose for a new pet?

Dear God,
Thank you for making people to be like you. I'm glad I can think and feel. Amen.

So God created human beings in his image. In the image of God he created them.   GENESIS 1:27

Adam's Wife, Eve

GENESIS 2:18-23

Have you ever felt lonely? Adam did. There were animals all around. But Adam was still lonely. He needed another person to be with him.

God didn't want Adam to be lonely. So he made a friend for Adam. She was the first woman. Her name was Eve. She became Adam's wife and friend. Eve was a special gift for Adam.

Who is your good friend?

Thank God for everyone in your family. He made them all!

Dear God,
You cared that Adam was lonely. I know that you care about how I feel too. Thank you for friends and families. Life is much happier because we have them.
Amen.

Then the LORD God formed a woman from the rib that he had taken from the man. GENESIS 2:22

22

God Rests When the Work Is Finished

GENESIS 2:1-3

At the end of a busy day, are you glad to go to bed? It feels good to rest when you are tired.

God finished making the world. He made the plants and trees, fishes and birds. He made the animals. He made the first man and the first woman. Everything was just the way God wanted it to be.

God was happy with everything he had made. So God stopped making things. He rested. God said we should rest on the seventh day of the week. That day would help us remember everything He made for us.

What do you do when you are tired?

Do you finish all your work before you rest?

Dear God,
Thank you for making the world just the way you wanted it to be. Thank you for not stopping in the middle. Thank you for making a rest day for us. Amen.

By the seventh day God had finished the work he had been doing. On the seventh day he stopped the work he had been doing.   GENESIS 2:2

Taking Care of God's World

Jamie and Mom were walking through the park on their way to the duck pond. "Mom, why are there so many cans and papers on the ground?" Jamie asked.

"Some people don't try to take care of the world God made for us," Jamie's mom answered. "They throw trash all around, even in the pond."

"Oh, is that why the water is so dirty that there are no fish any more?" Jamie asked.

Mom sighed, "Yes, Jamie. It is very sad. Each of us needs to help take care of the beautiful world God made for us."

How can you help take care of the world?

Can you plant some flowers to make the world more beautiful?

Dear God,
Adam took care of the world. I want to do that too. I will pick up trash I see in the park and put it in a trash can. Amen.

The LORD made the earth by his power. He set up the world by his wisdom. He stretched out heaven by his understanding.
JEREMIAH 51:15

God Is the Most Powerful

Sunday

God Shows His Power to Moses

EXODUS 4:1-5

God gave Moses a hard job to do. Moses did not think he could do it.

God's people were slaves in Egypt for a long time. Moses prayed for God to free them. God said Moses should lead the Israelites to freedom. But Moses was afraid. What if no one listened to him? What if he could not do it?

God said, "Throw your shepherd's staff down on the ground." When he did God turned it into a snake. Then God said, "Pick it up." Moses did, and it was a staff again. Now Moses knew that God's power would help him with the hard job.

When have you been afraid because of a hard job you had to do?

What can you ask God to help you with?

Dear God,
I am so glad to know about your power. Thank you that it will help me with anything that seems too hard for me. Amen.

The LORD will give power to his people.   PSALM 29:11

25

God Makes a King Listen to Him

Exodus 7:14–11:10

Some people always want to have their own way—even if it is not the right way. The king of Egypt was like that. God's people were his slaves. God wanted them to be free. So he sent Moses to tell the king. But the king kept saying, "No, they can't go!"

Ten terrible things happened to the Egyptian people because the king did not listen to God. The most terrible thing was the last thing that happened. The oldest child in every home died. The king wished he had listened to God. Now he knew that God is the most powerful.

How do you feel when a friend wants to have his or her own way?

Do you listen when Mom or Dad tells you to do something?

Dear God,
Help me remember that it is important to listen to you. Thank you for protecting me with your power. Amen.

"Hallelujah! Salvation, glory, and power belong to our God."

Revelation 19:1

God's People Escape

EXODUS 14

God's people were slaves in Egypt for many years. Now the king said they could leave. So Moses led them away. But when the king saw all his workers leaving, he changed his mind. He sent his army to bring them back.

The Israelites were trapped. The big Red Sea was in front of them and the Egyptian army was behind them. But God helped. He made the wind blow very hard. Soon the sea water blew into two big walls. There was a dry path in the middle. The Israelites walked through the Red Sea on a dry path! The Egyptian army chased them into the sea, but God made the water fall down on top of them.

How do you think the Israelites felt when the waters parted?

Has God's power ever kept you safe?

Dear God,
Thank you for keeping the Israelites safe. Thank you for keeping me safe too. Amen.

When the Israelites saw the great power the LORD had used against the Egyptians, they feared the LORD and believed in him and in his servant Moses.   EXODUS 14:31

The City of Jericho

JOSHUA 6:1-21

Joshua and his army wanted to capture Jericho. But there were big walls all around the city. How could they get over the walls?

God told Joshua to march his army around the city every day for seven days. "On the seventh day," God said, "march around it seven times. Blow your trumpets and shout. Then the walls will fall down."

Joshua obeyed God and the walls of the city fell down!

How do you think the people in Jericho felt when the army kept marching around their city?

How did Joshua feel when the walls fell down?

Dear God,
Joshua did what you said and the walls fell down. I'm glad your power is there to help me when I obey you too. Amen.

Love the LORD your God, follow his directions, and keep his commands.　　　JOSHUA 22:5

The Sun Stands Still

JOSHUA 10:1-13

Joshua once had a day that he did not want to end. Joshua's army was fighting an enemy that wanted to kill God's people.

Joshua's army was winning the battle. But it was almost dark. The battle would stop when it got dark and no one would be the winner. So Joshua asked God to make the sun stay up until his army won the battle.

God did it! He made the sun stand still for almost twenty-four hours! That is a whole day! Joshua's army won the battle.

Do you think Joshua said thank you to God?

When has God answered one of your prayers?

Dear God,
Thank you for listening to my prayers. Thank you for taking care of me. Amen.

The LORD is the strength of his people.　　　PSALM 28:8

29

Friday

God Is Better than Baal

1 KINGS 18:16-39

Some people do not believe God has the most power. Elijah met some men who thought their god, Baal, was more powerful than the real God. So they had a contest. The followers of Baal built an altar and put meat on it. Then they shouted and begged Baal to send down fire to burn it up. But nothing happened.

Then Elijah built an altar and put meat on it. He had water poured over it three times. Then Elijah asked God to send fire down to burn it. God did! The fire even dried up the water! God has the most power!

How do you think the followers of Baal felt when he didn't answer them?

Do you think Elijah was afraid? Why?

Dear God,
I do not need to ever be afraid. I can ask your help with anything I have to do. Thank you, God. Amen.

Be very careful to love the LORD your God. JOSHUA 23:11

A Scary Day

Jamie did not feel good when he woke up. Today was going to be a scary day . . . the first day of pre-school. Mom could not stay with him and he would not know anyone in the class.

"Jamie, are you feeling okay?" Mom asked. "You haven't said a word, and you aren't eating your breakfast."

Jamie burst into tears. "Mom, I'm scared to go to school. What if no one talks to me? What if I can't do what the teacher asks?"

Mom pulled him onto her lap.

"Jamie, let's ask God to help you. Remember he has the power to make kings listen to him and part the waters of a sea. He can help you be brave."

Do you think Jamie asked God to help him?
What would you like to ask God to help you with?

Dear God,
Thank you for caring about the things that make me afraid. Thank you for helping me be strong when I ask for your help. Amen.

I can do everything through Christ who strengthens me.

PHILIPPIANS 4:13

31

God Punishes Sin

The First Sin

GENESIS 3

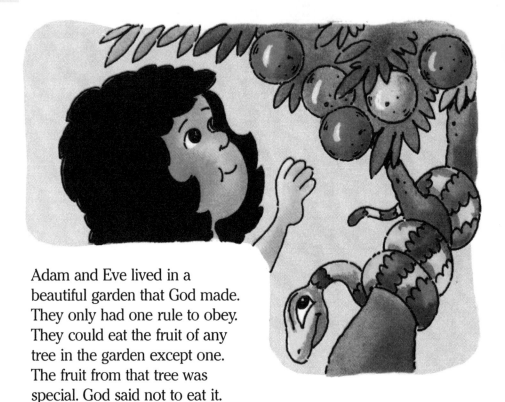

Adam and Eve lived in a beautiful garden that God made. They only had one rule to obey. They could eat the fruit of any tree in the garden except one. The fruit from that tree was special. God said not to eat it.

Adam and Eve did not obey God. They ate the special fruit.

Disobeying God is sin. God was sad that Adam and Eve did not obey him. He was sad because sin must be punished. God sent Adam and Eve out of the beautiful garden. Now they were sorry they disobeyed God.

Is there anyone who does not sin?

How do you feel when you do something wrong?

Dear God,
It is not easy to always obey. But I do not want to make you sad. Help me to obey. Amen.

All people have sinned and don't deserve any honor from God.

ROMANS 3:23

Two Brothers

GENESIS 4:1-13

Cain and Abel were brothers. Cain was a farmer and Abel was a shepherd. They both brought special offerings to God. God liked Abel's offering, but he did not like Cain's offering. God had given them rules about how to bring gifts to him. Cain did not obey the rules.

Cain got very angry that God did not like his gift. He was so angry that he killed Abel. Now God was very sad. He had to punish Cain. God said that the seeds Cain planted would not grow anymore. Also, Cain had to leave his home and wander around with no place to live.

What have you done when you were angry that you were later sorry for?

What is the best thing to do when you are angry?

Dear God,
I am sorry that I disobey sometimes. Help me learn what to do when I am angry. Help me to not hurt anyone because I am angry. Amen.

[Love] doesn't think about itself.

1 CORINTHIANS 13:5

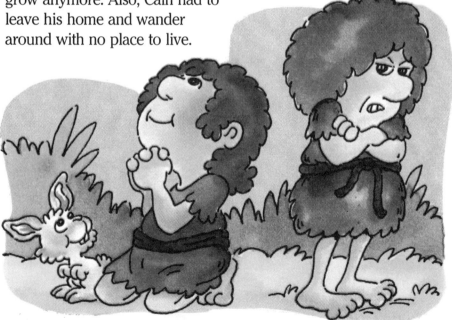

The World in Noah's Day

GENESIS 6:5-8; 7:23

Have you ever drawn a picture but been unhappy with the way it looked? Did you erase it and start over? God once did that.

God looked at how the people in his world were living. They were doing whatever they wanted. They did not even try to obey him. God was very sad. He decided to wipe the earth clean and start over.

Noah was the only man who obeyed God. So God saved Noah and his family. Everyone else was killed in the biggest flood ever. All because people didn't obey God.

What do you do when your friends want to do something wrong?

When have you been punished for doing something wrong?

Dear God,
Noah must have loved you very much. Other people probably made fun of him for obeying you. Help me to obey you, even when it is hard. Amen.

You are light for the world.

MATTHEW 5:14

The Tower of Babel

GENESIS 11:1-9

After the big flood, Noah and his family were the only people left on earth. Noah's sons had children and soon the earth was full of people again.

Then some people had an idea. "Let's build a tall tower," they said. "It will reach all the way to heaven. Everyone will think we are very important." They thought they were more important than God.

God did not like what these people were doing. He made them stop building the tower. Then he made each person speak a different language. Now they could not even talk to each other! No one should try to be more important than God.

These people were full of pride. Why does pride make God unhappy?

How do you feel when someone thinks they are more important than others?

Dear God,
Thank you for everything you help me do. Help me remember that I can do things only because you help me. Amen.

Pride precedes a disaster, and an arrogant attitude precedes a fall.
PROVERBS 16:18

35

A Golden Calf

Exodus 32:1-10

Moses was on a mountaintop praying to God. The Israelites were waiting for him to come down and lead them. But he was gone so long that they got tired of waiting.

They said to Aaron, "We don't think Moses is coming back. So God must be gone, too. Make us a god that we can see!" Aaron collected gold jewelry from the people. He melted it and shaped it into a golden calf. The people started worshiping the golden calf.

When God saw what they were doing, he was sad. They had forgotten everything he had done for them. Moses came back and destroyed the golden calf.

How would you feel if a friend forgot all the good times you had shared?

Is there something you enjoy so much that it is sometimes more important than God? What is it?

Dear God,
I don't want to let anything be more important than you in my life. Help me keep you first. Amen.

Never have any other god.
Exodus 20:3

The Strongest Man in the World

JUDGES 13–16

Samson was very strong. In fact, he was the strongest man who ever lived. Samson made a special promise to serve God. A sign of his promise was that he never cut his hair.

Samson's enemies made a deal with his friend, Delilah. They wanted her to find out why Samson was so strong. She asked Samson over and over about his strength.

Finally he told her that he was strong because his hair had never been cut. When Samson fell asleep, Delilah had a man cut his hair. Samson's promise to God was broken and his strength left. His enemies captured him.

When have you broken a promise?

How do you feel when someone breaks a promise to you?

Dear God,
Breaking a promise is sin and that meant Samson was punished. Help me to keep my promises. Amen.

You are my inheritance, O LORD. I promised to hold on to your words.   PSALM 119:57

Jamie Learns a Lesson

Jamie loved playing at Matt's house. Matt had neat toys. Jamie's favorite was a little silver airplane. The wings folded in and pressing a button on the bottom made the lights come on.

When it was time to go home, Jamie put the airplane in his pocket. He knew it was stealing, but he did it anyway.

At home, Mom saw Jamie playing with the airplane. "Where did you get that?" she asked. Jamie didn't answer. Mom asked again.

"It's Matt's," Jamie said softly.

"Does Matt know you have it?" Mom asked.

"No," Jamie answered.

"Jamie, I'm very sad that you took something that does not belong to you. You must give it back to Matt." Then Mom said, "I'm sorry, but I must punish you. You can not play with Matt for a whole week."

How do you think Jamie felt?

How are you punished for disobeying?

Dear God,
It is no fun to be punished. Help me to obey my parents and teachers. Most of all, help me to obey you. Amen.

Whoever has my commandments and obeys them is the person who loves me. John 14:21

38

God Is Our Helper

Sunday

Joseph Is Rescued

GENESIS 41:39-43

Joseph had a problem. A woman said he did something bad. He did not do it, but he was put in prison anyway.

One night the king of the land where Joseph was in prison had a dream. No one could tell the king what his dream meant. But one man knew that Joseph could help. God told Joseph what the dream meant. Joseph told the king. The king was very happy. He knew that God was helping Joseph. He put Joseph in charge of the whole country. One minute he was a prisoner, the next minute he was a ruler.

What has God helped you do?

When has someone been mean to you for no reason?

Dear God,
Sometimes life is not fair. I am glad to know that you will help me when I am in trouble. Amen.

I will strengthen you. I will help you.   ISAIAH 41:10

39

Food from Heaven

Exodus 16:1-16

God performed many miracles to help the Israelites escape from slavery in Egypt. Now they were walking through a desert on the way to their new home. But the people kept complaining, "We're hungry! We should have stayed in Egypt. We had all the food we wanted there. We're going to starve to death out here in the desert."

God heard them. He said to Moses, "I will send food." How could God do that? There was no food anywhere around.

But God did it. He made a special bread, called *manna*, fall down from the sky at night. Each person had enough food to eat every day.

How does it feel to be hungry?

Who gives you food?

Dear God,
It is so wonderful that you helped the hungry people even when they were complaining. Thank you for the food you give me.
Amen.

My God will richly fill your every need in a glorious way through Christ Jesus. Philippians 4:19

One Last Help for Samson

Judges 16:23-30

Samson was once the strongest man in the world. But when he disobeyed God his strength was taken away and the Philistines captured him. They did not believe in God. They were mean to Samson.

Samson was sorry for disobeying God. He asked God to help him one last time. He wanted to defeat the Philistines because they didn't love God. He was even willing to die with them if he had to.

God heard Samson's prayer and he gave his strength back. Samson pushed against the pillars that held up the building. It came crashing down on him and the Philistines. They all died. God helped Samson win one last time.

What do you need to say when you do something wrong?
Will God forgive you when you ask him to?

Dear God.
Thank you for forgiving me when I say I'm sorry. Thank you for helping me learn to be more like you. Amen.

The LORD is my strength.

Exodus 15:2

Wednesday

A Woman Gets Ready to Die

1 KINGS 17:7-16

Elijah went around teaching about God. One time God told him to go to Zarephath. A woman there would give him food.

When Elijah got to that town, he asked a woman for food and water. The woman sadly said, "I just have a little flour and oil to make one last meal for myself and my son. After that, we will starve to death."

Elijah said, "Don't worry. Go home and bake your bread. But first, make a small loaf for me. God will help you. He says your flour and oil will not run out." The woman did what Elijah said. God kept giving her flour and oil. She made all the bread she needed.

How did Elijah know God would help the woman?

How can you get God's help with a problem you have?

Dear God,
Thank you that you care about every problem I have, whether it is big or small. Help me remember that you will help me, if I just ask. Amen.

Ask, and you will receive. Search, and you will find. Knock, and the door will be opened for you.   MATTHEW 7:7

God Helps David

1 SAMUEL 17:1-50

Sometimes we all have to do things that are hard. Sometimes we are afraid.

When David was a young boy he had to do something that was hard. David may have been afraid. But he knew that God would help him. He knew that God was always with him.

David loved God. He wanted everyone to love God. Goliath was a giant Philistine. He did not love God. Goliath and his army were fighting the Israelite army. All the Israelites were afraid of Goliath. So David went by

himself to fight the giant. All David had to fight with was a slingshot and stones. David won! David may have been afraid, but he knew that God would help him.

How do you know God will never leave you alone?
Ask God to help you when you have to do something hard.

Dear God,
I'm so glad that you are always with me. Thank you for helping me when I have to do hard things. Amen.

I will never neglect you or abandon you. JOSHUA 1:5

43

You Do Not Have to Fight

2 CHRONICLES 20:1-29

Have you ever heard of an army winning a battle without even fighting? Jehoshaphat's army did.

A big army was coming to fight them. Jehoshaphat asked God for help. He told God that he remembered how powerful God is and how God had helped His people in the past.

God said, "Don't be afraid. You do not even have to fight this battle. Go down to meet the big army. But, do not fight; just stand there and see what God will do."

Jehoshaphat's army sang and praised God as they marched to the battle. Suddenly the enemy soldiers began fighting each other until they were all killed. God won the battle for his people!

How do you think Jehoshaphat's army felt as they marched toward the big army?

What big thing has God helped you with?

Dear God,
Thank you for stories in the Bible like this one. They help me remember that you will help me, if I just ask you to. Amen.

Don't be frightened or terrified . . . The LORD is with you."

2 CHRONICLES 20:17

I'm Lonely

Jamie sat on the front step drawing in the dirt with a stick. He was thinking about his friend Matt. He had so much fun with Matt. They played cars and airplanes and baseball. They had been best friends for as long as he could remember.

But now Jamie and his family lived in a new house in a new city. Dad got a new job so they had to move. "Jamie, why do you look so sad?" Mom asked as she sat down beside him.

"I miss Matt," Jamie said. "I wish we didn't have to move. I haven't got anyone to play with here."

"Well, honey, the best thing to do is ask God to send you a friend. Remember the stories in the Bible of how God helped people with their problems? Let's talk to him right now."

What do you think Jamie prayed?

Does God care when you are lonely?

Dear God,
Thank you for caring about my problems. I am glad that you care how I feel. Amen.

The Lord is my helper. HEBREWS 13:6

God Wants Us to Obey Him

Obedience Saves Noah

GENESIS 6:9–22

Noah loved and obeyed God. God was happy with Noah. God was not happy with everyone else. They did not try to obey Him. God told Noah that he was sending a big flood. The earth would be totally covered with water.

God told Noah to build a big boat called an ark. He told Noah to take two of every kind of animal on the ark. Noah did what God told him to do. Then it started to rain. It rained, and rained, and rained until the whole earth was flooded. Noah and his family and the animals were safe in the ark.

How do you think people felt when Noah built the big boat?

Was Noah glad that he had obeyed God?

Dear God,
I have a lot of people to obey.
Sometimes I get tired of obeying.
Help me to remember that
obeying makes you happy. Amen.

If you love me, you will obey what I tell you.   JOHN 14:15

Abraham Obeys

GENESIS 22:1-19

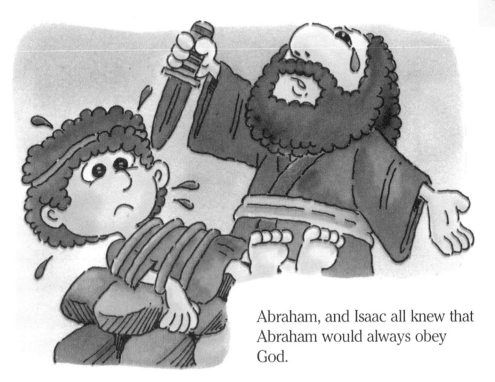

Abraham, and Isaac all knew that Abraham would always obey God.

One time obeying God was hard for Abraham. Abraham and his wife, Sarah, waited a long time for a baby. When their son Isaac was born they were very happy. Abraham loved Isaac very much. But then God asked Abraham to give Isaac to him as a sacrifice. That meant Isaac would die.

Abraham obeyed because he loved God. But, God stopped him before Isaac was hurt. Now God,

When was a time it was hard for you to obey?

Have you ever been unhappy that you obeyed?

Dear God,
Obeying is not always easy. It may mean giving up something that is important to me. Help me be strong enough to obey. Amen.

I am happy to do your will, O my God. Your teachings are deep within me. PSALM 4:8

47

Trust and Obey

DEUTERONOMY 1:8-46; NUMBERS 14:26-35

God promised to give the Israelites the land of Canaan. But, they did not trust God to keep his promise.

The Israelites sent twelve spies to see what Canaan was like. Ten of the spies came back afraid. They said the people who lived in Canaan were very big. "We could never defeat them," they said. The other two spies knew God would help them, because he had promised to give them the land.

But the people listened to the ten spies and gave up. They complained that they were going die out in the wilderness. The Israelites did not obey God. They did not go into Canaan. God made them walk around in the desert for 40 years. By then all the people who disobeyed God had died.

When have you complained instead of obeying?
What happens when you disobey?

Dear God,
Help me to believe your promises and trust what you say. I don't want to miss out on something good just because I disobey. Amen.

Be sure to obey the commands of the LORD your God and the regulations and laws he has given you.   DEUTERONOMY 6:17

Moses Loses His Temper

NUMBERS 20:6-12; DEUTERNOMY 3:21-29

Did you ever lose your temper because of how someone was acting? Moses was once punished for losing his temper.

Moses was leading the Israelites to the new land God had promised them. God did many miracles to help them. But every time things got a little bit tough, they started complaining. Now they were complaining because they were thirsty.

God told Moses to call the Israelites together. Then Moses should hold his shepherds staff in his hand, and speak to a big rock. When he did water would come pouring out of the rock.

But, Moses was tired of all their complaining and he lost his temper. Instead of speaking to the rock, he hit it with his staff. Moses disobeyed God. Now he would not be able to go into the Promised Land with the Israelites.

Why did Moses disobey God?

Is it ever alright to disobey?

Dear God,
Moses was very patient. But even disobeying one time meant he had to be punished. Help me remember that there is no excuse for disobeying, even one time. Amen.

Be careful to obey these laws. Then things will go well for you.

DEUTERONOMY 6:3

Rahab's Reward

JOSHUA 2; 6:22-23

Joshua sent two spies into Jericho. His army was going to try to capture the city, and he wanted to know more about it. The two men stayed at Rahab's house. She knew they were spies for Joshua. Rahab also knew their God was very powerful.

The king heard about the spies. He sent soldiers looking for them but Rahab hid the spies on the roof of her house. Then she told the soldiers that they had already left.

Later, when Joshua and his army captured Jericho, Rahab and her family were saved. This all happened because Rahab knew that the spies served God. She wanted to serve him, too.

Why do you think Rahab was so brave?

When have you had to do something hard to obey God?

Dear God,
It's easy to say I believe in you. But someday I may have to do something hard to prove that I do. Help me be brave. Help me remember that you will be with me. Amen.

In the same way let your light shine in front of people. Then they will see the good that you do and praise your Father in heaven.

MATTHEW 5:16

Jonah Obeys

JONAH

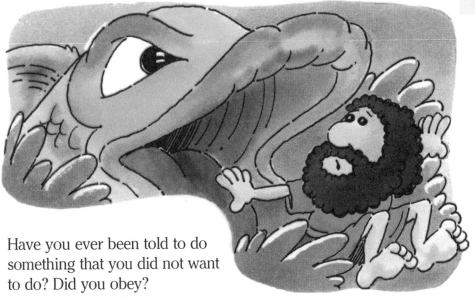

Have you ever been told to do something that you did not want to do? Did you obey?

God told Jonah to do something. But Jonah did not want to do it, so he ran away.

God wanted Jonah to go to Nineveh and tell the people there to obey God. Jonah did not want to go. He did not like the people in Nineveh. He did not want God to save them. So Jonah ran away.

God found a way to make Jonah listen to him. A big fish swallowed Jonah. He was inside the fish for three days. He had three days to think about disobeying God. When the fish spit him out, Jonah went to Nineveh and told the people to obey God. They did and God saved them.

Have you ever hidden so you did not have to obey?

Where can you hide from God?

Dear God,
Thank you for not giving up on Jonah when he disobeyed. I know you won't give up on me either.
Amen.

You, O Lord, are good and forgiving, full of mercy toward all who call out to you   PSALM 86:5

51

Jamie Disobeys

"Mom, can I go play at Ryan's house?" Jamie shouted down the stairs.

"No, Jamie. Ryan's house is too far for you to walk by yourself. But you may go next door to Tommy's," Mom answered.

Jamie thought about it for a minute. "OK," he said. But Jamie had a plan.

Mom went back to doing laundry as Jamie ran out the door. He crossed the driveway to Tommy's yard. But instead of going up to the door, Jamie kept going . . . across the yard, down the block, around the corner, all the way to Ryan's house.

When it was time for Jamie to come home, Mom called Tommy's house. She was surprised to find out Jamie wasn't there. A few phone calls later, Mom found Jamie at Ryan's house. She was very sad that Jamie had disobeyed her.

How do you think Jamie felt when he came home?
What do you think happened?

Dear God,
It is hard to obey. Being punished is no fun. Thank you that you will forgive me when I disobey.
Amen.

I have clung tightly to your written instructions. O LORD, do not let me be put to shame.
PSALM 119:31

God Is Our Protector

Sunday

Lot Is Saved

GENESIS 19:4-16

Moms and Dads take care of their children by protecting them and keeping them safe. God protects his children, too.

God protected Lot from danger. God decided to destroy the city of Sodom. The people who lived there did not love God and they did bad things. God was unhappy with them.

Lot and his family lived in Sodom and God wanted Lot to be safe. So before God destroyed the city, he sent angels to take Lot and his family out of Sodom. The city was destroyed, but Lot and his family were safe.

When was a time you were kept safe?
Who keeps you safe?

Dear God,
Thank you for keeping me safe.
Thank you for the grown-ups you gave me who keep me safe too.
Amen.

Turn to me and be saved, . . . because I am God, and there is no other. ISAIAH 45:22

Baby Moses Is Saved

GENESIS 2:1-10

God once protected Baby Moses. The Israelites were slaves in Egypt. The Egyptian king ordered that all the Israelite baby boys should be killed. He was afraid there were going to be too many Israelites in his land someday. They might try to take over.

But Moses' mother did not want her baby boy to die. She made a basket that would float in water. She put Baby Moses in the basket boat and floated him down the river.

An Egyptian princess saw the basket. She felt sorry for the little baby inside. She took the baby to the palace to live with her. When Moses grew up God used him to do wonderful things.

Why was the Egyptian king afraid of the Israelites?
Who protected Baby Moses?

Dear God,
Thank you that you are in control. It is good to know that you can take care of anything. Amen.

But let all who take refuge in you rejoice.   PSALM 5:11

The Passover
EXODUS 12:1-30

Everyone has rules to obey. When adults drive they must obey the rules of the road. There are rules at school and work. God gave some rules to the Israelites. If they obeyed the rules, they would be kept safe.

God wanted the Israelites to leave Egypt. He tried many ways to make the Egyptian king let the slaves leave. The king always said, "No!" The most terrible thing was going to happen now. The oldest child in every home would die. God told the Israelites how to protect themselves from this terrible thing. They did exactly what God told them to do and their children were all safe.

Would the Israelites have been safe if they had not done exactly what God said? How do you think the Egyptians felt about God?

Dear God,
Thank you for protecting the Israelites. Thank you for rules that keep us safe. Amen.

You are my hiding place. You protect me from trouble.

PSALM 32:7

Esther

ESTHER

Esther had to do something very hard. She had to trust God to help her.

Esther was the beautiful Queen of Persia. God used her to protect all the Jewish people. A bad man wanted to hurt the Jews. He did not like them. Esther was a Jew, but the king didn't know that. Esther had to tell the king what the bad man wanted to do. She had to tell him she was a Jew, also. The king might get very angry. He could have Esther killed.

But God wanted the Jews safe. He made the king listen to Esther. Her people were all saved. The bad man was punished.

Who helped Esther be brave?

Why were the Jews saved?

Dear God,
I am glad that you know everything that is going on. Thank you for helping Esther be brave. Thank you for protecting Esther and the Jews. Amen.

The LORD knows the way of righteous people.

PSALM 1:6

The Fiery Furnace

DANIEL 3

Sometimes people get in trouble even when they are doing the right thing. Shadrach, Meshach, and Abednego were in trouble because they would only worship God. The king of their land wanted all the people to worship a statue of him. Shadrach, Meshach, and Abednego said, "No, we will only worship God!"

The king got very angry. He had soldiers throw them into a fiery furnace. But God knew they had not done anything wrong. He protected them. They did not get burned at all. Now the king knew that God was the most powerful.

What would you do if someone said you had to worship someone other than God?

Would God protect you?

Dear God,
It isn't fair that Shadrach, Meshach, and Abednego were in danger. They were just being true to you. I'm glad you are in control, even when it looks like bad people are winning. Amen.

My help comes from the LORD, the maker of heaven and earth.

PSALM 121:2

57

Hungry Lions

DANIEL 6

Do you know someone who tries to get other people in trouble? That happened to Daniel. Some men tried to get him in trouble.

Daniel loved God and prayed to him every day. Bad men got the king to make a law that people could only pray to him. Daniel knew about the law, but he kept praying to God, right in his window where everyone could see him.

The king had Daniel thrown into a pit full of hungry lions. God protected Daniel. He kept the lions from eating him. The king was happy that Daniel was safe. He said everyone should pray to Daniel's God now.

Why do you think Daniel did not pray secretly, where no one could see him?

Did Daniel trust God to protect him?

Dear God,
Daniel was very brave because he trusted you. Help me be brave enough to stand up for you. Amen.

Be strong and courageous. Don't tremble! Don't be afraid of them! The LORD your God is the one who is going with you. He won't abandon you or leave you.

DEUTERONOMY 31:6

Ice Cream Danger

"Ice cream, ice cream. I love ice cream!" Jamie sang as he and Mom walked to the corner ice cream shop. Suddenly Jamie called out, "Race you, Mom!" and he took off running.

"Jamie, don't get so far ahead of me," called Mom. But Jamie paid no attention. He kept right on running.

Suddenly, Jamie saw that he was too close to the curb. He teetered on the edge of the busy street. Just as he was about to tumble into the street, a strong arm reached out and grabbed him.

"Thank you, Sir," Mom said as she ran up. The man made sure Jamie was okay. Then he went on his way.

How do you think Jamie felt?

Do you think Jamie thanked God for the man who caught him?

Dear God,
Mom and Dad try to protect me,
but sometimes I don't listen to
them. You want me to be safe
too. Thank you for taking care of
me. Thank you for my family
who help protect me. Amen.

The eternal God is your shelter, and his everlasting arms support you.

DEUTERONOMY 33:27

59

God Says How to Live

Only One God

Exodus 20:3

Sometimes people think there is something or someone that is more important than God. It may be their friends or a sports team. One of God's Ten Commandments is about that.

God told the Ten Commandments to Moses. Then Moses told the Israelites. Moses also wrote them down. They are in our Bibles so we can know how God wants us to live.

The very first commandment says that nothing should be more important to us than God.

What or who is most important to you?

How can you keep God important in your life?

Dear God,
I don't want to let anything become more important than you. Help me remember to talk to you every day. Amen.

Scripture says, 'You must worship the Lord your God and serve only him.' MATTHEW 4:10

Be Careful What You Say

EXODUS 20:7

Sometimes people use God's name in the wrong way. Instead of praising God, they say God's name as a swear word.

One of the Ten Commandments says this is wrong. God said, "You shall not misuse the name of the Lord your God." Anyone who uses God's name in the wrong way will be punished someday. We should remember that God is holy. We should only say his name in praise and love.

How do you feel when you hear God's name used as a swear word?

Do you ever think bad words, just because you hear them from other people?

Dear God,
I don't like to hear others use your name in the wrong way because I love you. Help me be careful about what I say and be a good example to my friends.
Amen.

The name of the LORD is a strong tower. A righteous person runs to it and is safe.   PROVERBS 18:10

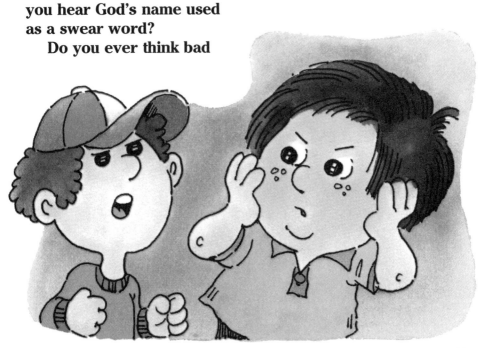

Tuesday

God Wants Us to Go to Church

EXODUS 20:8-11

Do you enjoy going to Sunday School and church? There is a good reason for you to go: God said you should.

The fourth commandment is, "Remember the Sabbath day by keeping it holy." On Sunday, you do not have school. Most people do not go to work. It is a day to rest and think about God. One way we keep the day holy is by going to church. At church and Sunday School we learn more about God. We think about God and worship him.

How can you make Sunday a special day?
How do you feel when Sunday morning comes?

Dear God,
Thank you for my Sunday School teacher and my minister. They study so they can teach me about you. Help me to pay attention in Sunday School and church.
Amen.

Remember the day of worship by observing it as a holy day.

EXODUS 20:8

Respect Your Father and Mother

EXODUS 20:12

Is it hard to obey your Mom or Dad? Obeying is important. But we all have trouble obeying sometimes. Number five of the Ten Commandments is: "Honor your father and your mother."

God said to obey your parents. You should treat them with respect. That means listening to them and obeying them. Obeying your parents helps you learn how to obey God. Your parents love you and want the best for you. So does God!

What is one way you can obey your parents?

How can you speak with respect to your parents?

Dear God,
Thank you for my parents. I am glad they love me and care for me. Help me to obey quickly when my parents ask me to do something. Amen.

Children, obey your parents because you are Christians. This is the right thing to do.

EPHESIANS 6:1

Be Careful How You Treat Others

EXODUS 20:13-16

thoughts in your mind. Taking something that belongs to someone else is stealing. Saying things that aren't true is lying. These things make God sad.

How does it feel to play with someone who is unkind? Four of God's Ten Commandments are about how to treat other people. "You shall not murder. You shall not commit adultery. You shall not steal. You shall not lie."

What do those words mean? You would never murder anyone. But this commandment means to try not to even get mad at others. Do not commit adultery means to keep pure. A good way to do that is be careful what you watch on TV. Some programs put bad

How do you feel when someone gets angry with you?

How you do feel when something of yours is stolen?

Dear God,
There are a lot of
commandments to remember.
Help me treat others the way I
would like to be treated. Amen.

Love your neighbor as yourself.
MATTHEW 19:19

Wanting What Someone Else Has

EXODUS 20:17

When one of your friends gets a new toy, do you wish you had one like it? Do you think about that toy all the time? Do you nag your parents to get you that toy? What you are doing is called coveting.

The last commandment is: "You shall not covet anything that belongs to your neighbor."

God said to be happy with what we have. He said to love each other. If we covet, we will fight with each other to get whatever we want. We won't have many friends then, will we?

What have you coveted? What other problems could come from coveting?

Dear God,
Sometimes I really want things that my friends have. But, I want to obey you. Help me to be happy with what I have, and to enjoy playing with my friends' toys. Amen.

Be content with what you have.
HEBREWS 13:5

Sunday Morning Blues

"Jamie, time to get up!" Mom called in a cheery voice.

"I'm too tired," Jamie mumbled.

"Come on. It's Sunday. We don't want to be late for Sunday School and church."

"I don't want to go. It's boring!" snapped Jamie. He pulled the covers over his head.

Mom sat down on his bed. "Jamie, remember the Ten Commandments? One of them says we should go to church. It doesn't have to be boring. Try listening to the Sunday school lesson. Ask questions and make sure you understand it. I am sure you can learn something about God today."

Do you think Mom's idea would work?

How do you feel about church?

Dear God,
Help me do my part on Sunday morning by listening to the lesson and asking questions when I do not understand. Amen.

My son, do not forget my teachings, and keep my commands in mind.

PROVERBS 3:1

God Has A Plan

Sunday

Bad Dreams, Good Dreams

GENESIS 37, 40–41

Bad things happen to everyone sometimes. When bad things happened to Joseph, he could have asked why God didn't stop the bad things. But Joseph knew God had a plan.

Joseph had a dream that his brothers were going to serve him someday. That dream did not make his brothers happy. They sold him to be a slave in Egypt. But Joseph ended up being a ruler. Being sold as a slave was part of God's plan to get Joseph to Egypt where he could make him a ruler.

How do you think Joseph felt when his brothers sold him to be a slave?

What bad thing would you like God to change?

Dear God,
When I hear about earthquakes or starving children, I wish you would do something. I am glad you have a plan for the whole world. I am glad you have a plan for my life. Amen.

The LORD's plan stands firm forever. PSALM 33:11

67

Joseph Saves His Family

GENESIS 42, 45

If you had the chance to help someone who had been mean to you, would you?

Joseph did. His brothers sold him to be a slave in Egypt. Many years later, they came to Egypt looking for food. Their whole family would starve if they did not find some. The man they had to ask for food was their brother, Joseph. But they did not know that.

Joseph could say no to them. He could send them home to starve. But Joseph knew that being able to help his family was part of God's plan for him. He was happy to do what God wanted him to do.

Do you know any of God's plan for you?

How do you think Joseph felt when his brothers asked him for food?

Dear God,
Joseph did the right thing by helping his brothers. Help me be strong enough to do the right thing in a hard situation. Amen.

Share what you have with God's people who are in need.

ROMANS 12:13

Ruth and Naomi

RUTH

God is in control of everything. But it may have been hard for Ruth and Naomi to remember that. Naomi's family moved to Moab because there was no food in their land. Ruth married Naomi's son. When their husbands died, Naomi wanted to go home to Judah. Ruth went with her. But they had no money or food. How would they live?

Ruth picked up left-over grain in a field owned by Boaz. She used it to make bread. Since Boaz liked Ruth he told the workers to drop extra grain on the ground for her.

Soon Ruth and Boaz were married. Many years later a member of their family was God's Son, Jesus.

How do you think Ruth and Naomi felt when they got to Judah?
When have you had trouble waiting to see what God's plan is?

Dear God,
Sometimes it takes a long time to understand your plan. Help me be patient enough to trust you. Help me keep trusting you. Amen.

Wait with hope for the LORD. Be strong, and let your heart be courageous. Yes, wait with hope for the LORD.   PSALM 27:14

69

Nehemiah's Sadness

NEHEMIAH 2

When you have a job to do, are you happy to do it? Even if it is a hard job? Nehemiah was. He had a very important job to do. He felt bad that God's holy city, Jerusalem, was falling down in ruins. Nehemiah didn't think it was good for God's city to look that way.

Nehemiah took a group of people to Jerusalem to rebuild the walls around the city. Then everyone would know God was still in control. Nehemiah did the first step of God's plan to make Jerusalem a strong city again.

What hard job have you had to do?

What can you do that shows honor to God?

Dear God,
Doing hard jobs for you doesn't seem very likely since I am just a kid. But I want to be part of your plan in any way that I can. Help me to be part of your work. Amen.

God, who began this good work in you, will carry it through to completion on the day of Christ Jesus.   PHILIPPIANS 1:6

Daniel and the King's Dream

DANIEL 2

Sometimes God helps a person do something special. Then he uses that special thing in his plan.

God helped Daniel understand what some dreams meant. Then one night the king had a dream he did not understand. He asked his wise men to explain it, but none of them could. Daniel was the only one who could tell the king what his dream meant.

The king was so happy to know what his dream meant, that he made Daniel a ruler in the land. That was just what God planned. Now Daniel was right where God wanted him to be.

What dream do you remember having?

What special thing does God help you do?

Dear God,
Sometimes I do not feel like I can do anything special. Help me to think about the things I like to do. Those things are special. Use my special things in your plan. Amen.

Teach me to do your will.

PSALM 143:10

Friday

David Is Chosen

1 Samuel 16:1-13

It feels good to be chosen for a team or a part in a program. David was once chosen for something very special.

God was unhappy with the disobedient king of Israel. God wanted a new king.

God told Samuel that one of Jesse's sons would be the new king. Seven of Jesse's sons came to Samuel. One was very handsome. One was very tall. Each time Samuel thought he had found the new king, God said no. Soon, there were no sons left for Samuel to see.

The boy who would be the new king was taking care of the sheep. Samuel called him. When young David came, God said, "This is the boy who will be king." That was God's plan.

Why did Samuel think the tall son or the handsome son should be king?

Why do you think God chose David?

Dear God,
Thank you for helping Samuel find the right boy. Help me to be patient when I am waiting to see what you want. Amen.

O LORD, our Lord, how majestic is your name throughout the earth!
PSALM 8:1

Game Plans

Jamie loved basketball. Tonight he was going to a pro basketball game for the first time!

As Jamie watched, he was surprised at how fast the players ran up and down the court.

"Dad, how do the players know where everyone is going to be? They throw the ball without even looking," Jamie said.

"Because they have learned plays," said Dad.

"What is a play?" asked Jamie.

"It's like a plan," answered Dad. "The coach plans how each player will move around the court. Then everyone knows where their teammates will be."

"That is just like God. He has a plan for the world," Jamie remembered. "He knows everything that is going to happen. He is never surprised by anything."

Have you ever made plans for something?
What did you learn about God's plan this week?

Dear God,
I am glad that you know
everything that is going to happen.
Thank you that you have a plan
for my life. Amen.

In all your ways acknowledge him, and he will make your paths smooth.   PROVERBS 3:6

God Gives Us Families

Sunday

The First Babies

GENESIS 4:1-2

Do you have brothers and sisters? Do you have a grandmother and grandfather? Do you enjoy it when your whole family is together?

Adam and Eve were the first people God made. They did not bump into other people on the street. They did not have to wait in line to do things. They were the only two people on earth. But they also did not have friends or family to be with.

God told Adam and Eve to have children. He wanted the world to be full of people. Soon Adam and Eve had two baby boys. Cain and Abel were the first babies born on earth.

How many people are in your family?

Look for a picture of you when you were a baby.

Dear God,
Thank you for my family. Even when I fight with them, I do not stop loving them. Thank you for making families. Amen

Children are an inheritance from the LORD. They are a reward from him.   PSALM 127:3

The Miracle Baby

GENESIS 21:1-7

Have you ever had to wait a long time for something? Waiting is hard. Abraham and Sarah knew that. For a very long time, they wanted to have a baby. They asked God over and over. He always said, "Yes." But they still did not have a baby.

Now Abraham and Sarah were very old. They were tired of waiting, so they gave up on ever having a baby. That's when God gave them one.

When their son Isaac was born, Abraham and Sarah praised God. They were very happy. Their precious baby was worth waiting for.

What have you waited for a long time to happen?

How do you feel when you have to wait?

Dear God,
Abraham and Sarah must have been so excited. But waiting is not easy. Thank you that when you say something is going to happen, it does, even if we have to wait for it. Amen.

Every good present and every perfect gift comes from above, from the Father who made the sun, moon, and stars.   JAMES 1:17

75

A Bride for Isaac

GENESIS 24

Doesn't it feels good to know someone loves you? It is nice to have a family to love and to comfort you when you are sad.

Abraham's son, Isaac, was grown up and ready to get married. But, Abraham did not want him to marry a girl from nearby because those people didn't love God. So Abraham sent a servant back to their land, Israel, to find a wife for Isaac.

The servant prayed that God would lead him to the right girl for Isaac. God did. He led the servant to Rebekah.

The servant brought Rebekah home to Isaac. He was very happy to see her. Rebekah and Isaac loved each other. They were soon married.

Name some people who love you.

Did God care which girl Isaac married?

Dear God,
Thank you for caring when I am lonely. Thank you for my family. Amen.

The LORD grants favor and honor. He does not hold back any blessing from those who live innocently. PSALM 84:11

Fighting Brothers

GENESIS 25:19-26

Do you have a brother or sister? Do you ever fight with them? Most brothers and sisters do fight sometimes. But not as bad as Jacob and Esau.

Jacob and Esau were twin brothers. But they did not get along with each other. Part of the problem was that their father, Isaac, liked Esau best and their mother, Rebekah, liked Jacob best. Their fighting ended when Jacob stole something from Esau. Esau was so angry that he wanted to kill his brother. So Jacob ran away from home. The two brothers did not see each other for a long time.

What do you fight about with your brothers or sisters?

How do you feel when you fight with a family member or a friend?

*Dear God,
Even though I fight with my brothers and sisters, I would be very sad not to see them for a long time. Help me to be more patient and less selfish when I am with my brothers and sisters. Amen.*

Share the same attitude and live in peace.   2 CORINTHIANS 13:11

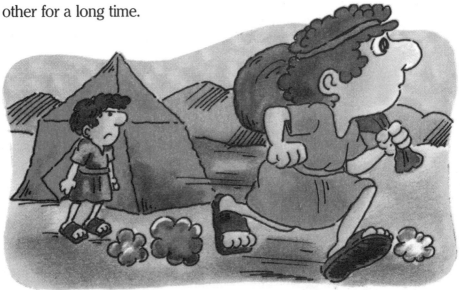

Big Sister Babysits

Exodus 2:4, 7

Do you have an older brother or sister who babysits you? There was one sister who took good care of her baby brother, Moses.

God used Moses to do many important things when he grew up. But Moses almost did not get to grow up.

When Moses was a baby, a bad king wanted all the baby boys to die. Moses' mother had a plan to protect him. But his sister, Miriam, had to help. She hid by a river and watched as Moses floated in a basket. When a princess found the baby, Miriam asked if she wanted someone to care for him. The princess said yes, so Miriam ran to get her mother. Moses was safe and had his own mother to care for him.

How do you think Miriam felt about watching Moses?

How do you feel when your brother or sister babysits you?

Dear God,
Thank you for older brothers and sisters. They are fun to have around. Amen.

I pray that God, the source of hope, will fill you with joy and peace through your faith in him.

Romans 15:13

Long Awaited Child

1 SAMUEL 1

Have you ever wanted something so much that you could not think about anything else? Hannah did. She wanted a baby and she could not think about anything else. Hannah asked God to give her a baby. But, she did not have a child yet.

Hannah cried and cried and asked God to please give her a baby. She even promised God that if he would give her a baby she would give the child back to God to serve him.

God did give Hannah a baby boy. She named him Samuel. Hannah was very happy to have a son. She kept her promise to God and gave Samuel to serve God.

What have you wanted so much that you asked for it over and over?
Why do you think Hannah wanted a baby so much?

Dear God,
Thank you for answering Hannah's prayer. Thank you that you listen when I pray, too.
Amen.

My heart finds joy in the LORD.
1 SAMUEL 2:1

Family Reunion

Jamie was so excited that he thought he would burst! Only two more weeks until the family reunion. Jamie's family was going to Missouri where Jamie would see his aunts, uncles, cousins, and grandparents.

Jamie was most excited about seeing his cousin, Billy. They were almost the same age and they always had fun together. Jamie planned what toys to take along. Did Billy like baseball, jet planes, or video games? Mom suggested that Jamie write to Billy and ask him.

Mom got out the photo album with pictures from the last family reunion. They looked at it together and Jamie went to sleep that night with the photo album tucked under his arm.

Have you ever been to a family reunion?

Where do your grandparents or aunts and uncles live?

Dear God,
Thank you for each member of my family. Being in a family makes me feel safe and secure. Thank you that I am part of your family too. That is even more special! Amen.

Let us come into his presence with a song of thanksgiving.
PSALM 95:2

God Gives Strength

Crossing the Jordan

JOSHUA 3

Joshua was the new leader of the Israelites. Moses had led them for a long time and the people liked Moses. Would they like Joshua? Would they trust him?

God wanted to show the people that he would help Joshua, just as he had helped Moses. God told Joshua, "Have the priests stand in the middle of the Jordan River. Tell the people to watch what happens."

When the priests stepped into the river, the water divided into two big walls on either side. The people walked through the Jordan River on dry land.

Now everyone knew that God's strength was helping Joshua.

How do you think the people felt when they knew God was helping Joshua?

How have you seen God's strength in your life?

Dear God,
Your strength helps me every day. It makes me feel safe. Thank you for taking care of me. Amen.

God arms me with strength. His perfect way sets me free.

2 SAMUEL 22:33

81

Deborah and Barak

JUDGES 4:6-15

How do you feel when someone is mean to you? Do you want to get away from them?

The Israelites were slaves, and the slavemaster was very mean to them. So they wanted to get away. God told Deborah and Barak to lead an army to fight for the Israelites' freedom. He said he would help them.

Deborah and Barak led their little army to fight the bigger, more powerful army. The Lord made the enemy army get scared and run away. God's strength won the battle.

How do you think Deborah and Barak felt?

How does God take care of you?

Dear God,
You always take care of your people. There are many stories in the Bible about when you did that. Thank you that you take care of me. Amen.

The LORD is my rock, my fortress and my Savior. PSALM 18:2

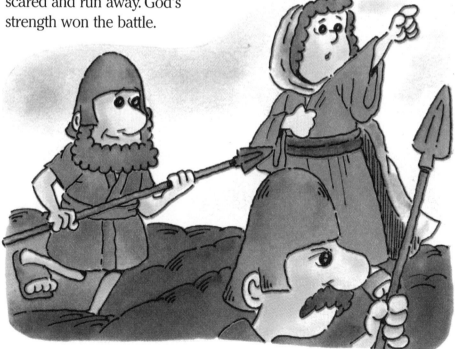

Gideon's Little Army

JUDGES 7:1-22

God told Gideon to lead his army to fight the Midianites, who were a big powerful enemy. Gideon gathered an army of 32,000 soldiers. God wanted everyone to know that Gideon's army would win because of God's strength. They would not win because of how big their army was. So Gideon sent 22,000 soldiers home. God said there were still too many soldiers. God cut Gideon's army down to 300 soldiers. Gideon's army won! Everyone knew God's strength won the battle.

How do you think Gideon felt when God cut his army down to 300 soldiers?

Has God helped you with a big problem?

Dear God,
There is nothing you cannot do!
You helped Gideon win with a
little army. I know you can take
care of me whatever happens!
Amen.

Be strong, all who wait with hope for the LORD, and let your heart be courageous.   PSALM 31:24

Ruth Leaves Home

RUTH 1:16-17

How would you feel if you had to move away from your family and the only home you had ever lived in? That would be hard to do, wouldn't it?

Ruth moved away from the home where she grew up. She left her family and the friends she had always known. Why did she do it? Ruth wanted to go to Judah with Naomi. Ruth wanted to serve Naomi's God. Ruth knew it was the right thing to do. God helped her be strong enough to leave home and go to Judah.

Who would you miss if you moved to a new home?

What do you need God's strength to help you with?

Dear God,
It must have been hard for Ruth to leave her home. But Ruth knew that was the right thing to do. Help me be strong enough to do the right thing. Amen.

Wherever you go, I will go, and wherever you stay, I will stay. Your people will be my people, and your God will be my God.

RUTH 1:16

84

David Spares Saul's Life

1 SAMUEL 24

If someone had been mean to you for a long time, would you want a chance to get even with him?

Saul was king of Israel. But he was very mean to David because he was jealous of him. Saul chased David and tried to kill him many times.

Then one night, David found Saul sleeping in a cave. There was no one guarding him. This was David's chance to kill Saul. But David knew that was the wrong thing to do. Saul was the king and David should not kill him. God helped David do the right thing. He helped David be strong.

When has someone been mean to you?

Why would it have been wrong for David to hurt Saul?

Dear God,
Thank you for the strength to do the right thing. Thank you for helping David. And thank you for helping me. Amen.

The LORD is my rock . . . in whom I take refuge.   PSALM 18:2

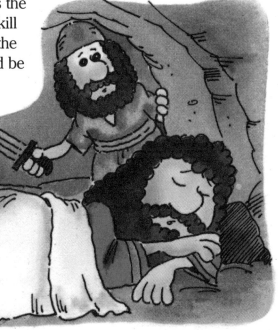

Friday

David Becomes King

2 SAMUEL 5:1–5

Would you like to know now what job you will have when you are grown up?

David knew what he would be. God chose David to be king of Israel when David was just a boy. When King Saul died, David did become king, just as God promised. Many armies fought against David's army. But David trusted God. God helped him win many battles. God helped David be kind to people. God promised David that he would help him protect the Israelites from their enemies. God's strength helped David be a good king.

How do you think David felt when he was chosen to be king?

Do you think God has a special plan for your life?

*Dear God,
There were many times when David had to fight his enemies. You helped him every time. Thank you that you will help me when I ask you to. Amen.*

Be courageous and strong.

1 CORINTHIANS 16:13

I'm Scared

Jamie had a speaking part in the Sunday School program. He would say his lines in front of the whole church. Jamie practiced saying the lines loudly. He practiced saying them softly.

On program day, Jamie dressed in his best clothes. He combed his hair nice and smooth. He practiced his lines in front of the mirror. Then he rode to church with Mom and Dad. When they drove into the parking lot, Jamie started to cry.

"What's the matter?" Mom asked.

"I'm scared. I don't want to talk in front of the whole church," Jamie cried.

"Calm down," Dad said. "Remember the stories in the Bible about God helping people

be strong. He will help you too. Let's ask him."

What do you think Jamie prayed?

What do you need God's strength to help you with?

Dear God,
Sometimes I am afraid. Sometimes I need your help to be strong. Thank you for helping me when I ask. Amen.

God our Father loved us and by his kindness gave us everlasting encouragement and good hope.

2 THESSALONIANS 2:16

God Is Always with You

God Remembers Noah

GENESIS 8

Sometimes things happen that are hard to understand. A person may feel that God has forgotten about him. Noah may have wondered about things that were happening. But Noah knew God would not forget about him.

Noah was in a big boat. He had been in the boat for a long time. The whole earth was covered by a big flood. God put Noah in the boat because he obeyed God. He kept Noah safe. The flood lasted a long time. When the flood was over, God told Noah it was safe to come out of the boat. God did not forget about Noah.

How do you know God will never forget about you?
How do you know that God will never leave you?

Dear God,
Thank you that you never leave me. When I am afraid, help me remember that you are with me. Amen.

Give thanks to the LORD because he is good, because his mercy endures forever. PSALM 106:1

Jacob's Dream

GENESIS 28:10-22

Are you afraid to be alone? Are you scared when you are in your dark bedroom by yourself?

Jacob was alone. He left his family behind and went to a new land. He may have been afraid. He did not know what was going to happen to him.

Then Jacob had a dream. In the dream God told him some things that were going to happen in the future. God said he would always be with him. Now Jacob was not afraid.

What makes you afraid? How do you think Jacob felt after God talked to him?

Dear God,
I do not like to be by myself. I feel better when other people are with me. I am glad that you are always with me. Amen.

The LORD is your guardian.

PSALM 121:5

Joseph

GENESIS 39:20-23

When bad things happen it may be hard to remember that God is with you. If you are being treated unfairly, you may not feel like God is with you.

God was with Joseph when he was treated unfairly. Joseph had not done anything wrong. But he was in prison. God helped the warden see that Joseph was a good person. The warden treated Joseph kindly. He put Joseph in charge of all the other prisoners.

When was a time that you were treated unfairly?

How did you feel when you were treated unfairly?

Dear God,
It hurts to be treated unfairly. Help me remember to talk to you about how I feel when I am treated that way. Thank you that you know everything that is happening to me. Amen.

The LORD reached out to [Joseph] with his unchanging love and gave him protection.　　GENESIS 39:21

Clouds and Fire

Exodus 13:21-22

Sometimes it is not enough just to *know* that God is with you. Sometimes you need to *see* something that shows he is there.

The Israelites needed to see that God was with them. They had been slaves in Egypt for forty years. Now they were free and starting the trip to their home in a new land. God knew they were scared. So he sent a cloud that led them all day. At night it became a tall column of fire. The Israelites just had to look up to see that God was with them.

When have you wished that you could see proof that God was with you?

How do you know that God is always with you?

Dear God,
Thank you that you promised in the Bible to always be with me. Help me remember that you are with me, even if I can't see you. Amen.

Whoever lives under the shelter of the Most High will remain in the shadow of the Almighty.

Psalm 91:1

Thirsty People

EXODUS 15:22-25

If someone is hungry or thirsty, it may be hard for him to remember that God is with him.

The Israelites were going to the land God promised to give them. They had been walking in a hot dry desert for three days, so they were hot and thirsty. But the only water they could find was very bitter. God was with them though. He heard them saying they were thirsty. So God told Moses to throw a tree into the water. When he did the water became sweet. The Israelites could drink all they wanted.

When was the last time you were very thirsty?

Does God care about things like whether you are thirsty?

Dear God,
Thank you that I can talk to you about anything that worries me. You care about everything that matters to me. Amen.

Our help is in the name of the LORD, the maker of heaven and earth.   PSALM 124:8

A New Leader

JOSHUA 1:1-5

Moses led the Israelite people for many years. God did many miracles to show the people he was with Moses. Now Moses was dead. Joshua was their new leader. Would God help Joshua too?

God himself chose Joshua to be the new leader of the people. He told Joshua that he would help him, just as he had helped Moses. He told Joshua he could be strong and brave because he would know that God was with him wherever he went.

When you get a new teacher or club leader, do you still think about your old teacher?

How do you think Joshua felt after God promised to be with him?

Dear God,
Thank you for being with Joshua, as you were with Moses. Thank you for telling him you were with him. Thank you that you are always with me too. Amen.

Be strong and courageous! Don't tremble or be terrified, because the LORD your God is with you wherever you go.　　JOSHUA 1:9

The Dark Room

"Good night, Jamie. Sleep well," Mom said as she kissed Jamie on the forehead.

"See you tomorrow, buddy. I love you," said Dad, turning out the light.

When Mom and Dad had closed the door, Jamie looked around his dark bedroom. The moonlight coming through the window made shadows on the wall. Jamie started to get scared. Just when he was ready to call for Mom and Dad, Jamie remembered the Bible stories his family had read together that week. Jamie remembered that he was not alone. God was with him.

What makes you feel afraid?
What can you do when you are afraid?

Dear God,
Help me remember that you are always with me. I do not need to be afraid of anything. Help me remember to talk with you when I am afraid. Amen.

I am always with you.
MATTHEW 28:20

94

God Is Love

Sunday

Best Friends

1 SAMUEL 20

David and Jonathan were best friends. But they had a problem. Jonathan's father was King Saul. King Saul did not like David. He thought the people wanted David to be king instead of him.

David hid while Jonathan went to see how angry King Saul was. He found out that his father wanted to kill David. Jonathan ran to tell David. They were very sad. They had to say good-bye. David and Jonathan knew they would never see each other again. But they promised to always be friends.

Who is your best friend? Did you know that God wants to be your very best friend?

Dear God,
Thank you for friends. They make life so much more fun. Thank you that you want to be my best friend. I love you. Amen.

Love each other. This is what I'm telling you to do.   JOHN 15:17

Loving Your Enemies

2 SAMUEL 9

King Saul hated David. He chased David and tried to kill him. Finally King Saul died. David was glad that he did not have to hide from Saul anymore.

Now David became king. He asked his servant to find out if there were any relatives of King Saul still alive. David wanted to be nice to them. There was only one of Saul's family members still alive. He was a crippled man named Mephibosheth. David brought Mephibosheth to the palace. He shared everything he had with Mephibosheth.

How do you think Mephibosheth felt when David called for him?

How do you treat people who have been mean to you?

Dear God,
David showed that he loved you by being kind to a member of his enemy's family. I want people to know that I love you too. Help me show your love to my enemies. Amen.

Love your enemies, and pray for those who persecute you.

MATTHEW 5:44

Elijah's Reward

2 KINGS 2:1-11

Elijah was a prophet. He told people about God. Elijah always tried to serve God. He talked about God even when people got angry at him for it because he loved God. Now it was time for Elijah to go to heaven. His work on earth was finished.

God took Elijah to heaven in a special way. He wanted to reward Elijah's hard work and service. So God sent a chariot that was made of fire and pulled by horses. Elijah got in and rode to heaven in a big wind.

How do you think Elijah felt when he saw the chariot of fire?

How did Elijah show that he loved God?

Dear God,
I am glad that you rewarded Elijah. He worked hard for you. Thank you for loving your children. Thank you for loving me. Amen.

Rejoice and be glad, because you have a great reward in heaven!
MATTHEW 5:12

97

Help for a Widow

2 Kings 4:1-7

Elisha met a woman who had a problem. When her husband died, he owed a man a lot of money. Now that man was going to take her sons to be slaves. That would be payment for the debt. The woman had no money to pay the man. In fact, all she had was a little oil in a jar.

Elisha told her to get all the jars she could find and pour her oil into them. God did a miracle! The oil kept coming and coming. Soon all the jars were filled. Now the woman could sell the oil. She could pay the man and her sons would be free.

How did the woman know that God loved her?

How do you know God loves you?

Dear God,
Thank you for helping the lady. It would have been sad for her to lose her sons. Thank you for helping me with the problems I have everyday. Amen.

Turn your burdens over to the LORD, and he will take care of you.   Psalm 55:22

Showing Love to God

1 Chronicles 22:6-7; 2 Chronicles 2-3

When you love someone you want to do kind things for them. You want to give them gifts and make them feel special.

David loved God. He wanted to build a beautiful temple for God. God said David could make all the plans, but he should not build it. David's son, Solomon, would finish the project. Solomon got many workers to build the temple. He ordered special wood from another country. He used silver, gold, beautiful cloth, and bronze to build a beautiful house for God.

What does your church look like?

What gift could you give God?

Dear God,
I can show I love you. I can be kind to my brothers or sisters. I can help take care of my church. I can sing songs about you. Thank you that there are ways I can show my love for you. Amen.

The LORD's glory filled God's temple.

2 Chronicles 5:14

99

Friday

Unexpected Love

EZRA 1:5-11

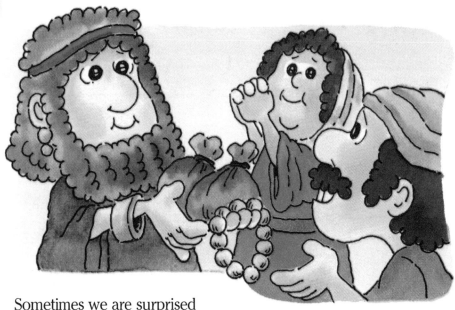

Sometimes we are surprised when a person who is different from us shows that he loves God. Sometimes we forget that God loves everyone, not only people who are just like us.

King Cyrus was king of Persia. He was not known as someone who loved God. But God helped him understand that everything he had was a gift from God.

King Cyrus wanted to do something for God. So he sent the Israelites back to their own land. He helped them rebuild God's temple that had been torn down in a battle.

King Cyrus gave gold and silver trays, gold and silver bowls, and many other things for the temple.

Who can you think of that may not love God?
Will you tell that person that God loves him?

Dear God,
Thank you for loving everyone. Help me remember not to judge people by how they look or where they live. Amen.

God is love.   1 JOHN 4:8

Jamie Shows Love

Jamie and Matt were walking past the house where a new family lived. The people had moved in a week ago, but Jamie had not met them yet. He knew there was a boy about his age because he had seen him sitting on the steps when he and Matt walked by once before.

Sure enough, as Jamie and Matt got close to the house they saw the boy sitting on the steps. He looked lonely. "Hey, there's that new kid. Let's cross the street so we don't have to talk to him," Matt whispered. The two friends hurried across the street. But, as they passed the house, Jamie stopped.

"Matt, that boy looks lonely. Let's see if he wants to play with us," Jamie said. And he ran across the street.

How did Jamie show love? To whom could you show love today?

Dear God,
Help me remember that you love
me. Help me be brave enough to
tell others that you love them too.
Amen.

We must show love through actions that are sincere, not through empty words.

1 JOHN 3:18

God Gives Wisdom

God Helps Joseph

GENESIS 41:1-39

Have you ever had a strange dream? Did you wonder what it meant? The king of Egypt had two dreams that he did not understand. He asked all his counselors and wise men what the dreams meant. No one could tell him.

Then someone remembered a prisoner named Joseph who could explain dreams. The king sent for Joseph. Joseph loved God. God helped Joseph explain the dreams.

The king said that since Joseph was so wise he should help rule the country. He would be second only to the king.

What dream do you remember having?

How do you get wisdom from God?

Dear God,
Joseph would not have been able to explain the dreams if he had not been close to you. Help me know you better so I can be wise too. Amen.

God's riches, wisdom, and knowledge are so exceptional that it is impossible to explain his decisions or to understand his ways!

ROMANS 11:33

Teach Your Children

DEUTERONOMY 11:19-21; 32:47

How do you learn things? Probably you are taught by your parents, Sunday School teachers, or school teachers.

Moses knew how important it is to teach children. He knew that children need to learn how God wants them to live. The best way they can learn what God wants is for their parents to teach them.

God knows that the best way for children to learn about him is at home. Parents can teach about God through things that happen everyday.

What things have your parents taught you?

Why does God want you to know what the Bible says?

Dear God,
Help me listen to Mom and Dad. I will learn more about how to live for you by listening to my parents. Amen.

Love the LORD your God, follow all his directions, and be loyal to him.

DEUTERONOMY 11:22

Abigail

1 SAMUEL 25:1-35

Being wise means showing good judgment and making wise decisions. Abigail showed wisdom and good judgment. She kept David from making a big mistake.

David was going to kill a man named Nabal. Nabal had been mean to David. He said mean things to David even after David had been kind to Nabal and protected him.

Abigail was Nabal's wife. When she heard how mean Nabal had been, she hurried to see David. She brought gifts to him. She begged him to forgive Nabal's rudeness. She said it would be wrong for David to kill Nabal.

David knew she was right. He thanked her and accepted the gifts. He did not kill Nabal.

What decisions do you have to make every day?

How do you think Abigail felt as she went to see David?

Dear God,
Help me to make wise choices.
That will show that I am learning more about how to live for you.
Amen.

The fear of the LORD is the beginning of knowledge.

PROVERBS 1:7

Solomon's Wise Choice

1 KINGS 3:5-13

If God said you could have anything you wanted, what would you ask for? Would it be hard to decide?

God told Solomon to ask for anything he wanted. He could have asked to be rich and famous. He could have asked to be the most powerful man on earth. But Solomon did not ask for any of those things. He asked that God make him wise enough to tell the difference between good and evil.

God was happy with Solomon's choice. So he made Solomon wise, and he also made him rich and famous.

Is it always easy to know what is right and what is wrong?

Why was God happy with what Solomon asked for?

Dear God,
I don't know if I would have asked for wisdom. Help me learn to make good choices in how I live and what I pray for. Amen.

The LORD gives wisdom. From his mouth come knowledge and understanding.   PROVERBS 2:6

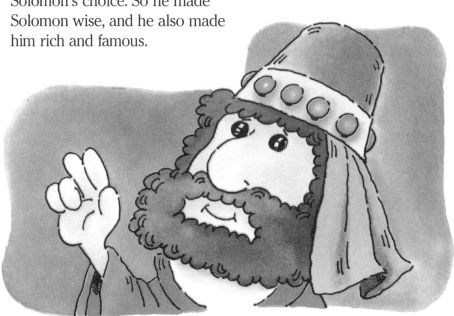

Solomon Uses His Wisdom

1 KINGS 3:16-28

Have you ever tried to settle an argument between two people? Sometimes it is hard to know who is right and who is wrong.

Solomon asked God for wisdom and God gave it to him. Now Solomon had to use his wisdom. Two mothers came to him, each claiming that a little baby was theirs.

Solomon knew what to do. He said to cut the baby in half and give half to each mother. Solomon knew the real mother would not want that to happen. When one woman shouted, "NO!" Solomon knew she was the real mother.

When have you had to decide who was telling the truth?

How did Solomon know what to do?

Dear God,
Thank you for helping Solomon know what to do. Please give me wisdom when I have hard choices to make. Amen.

Whoever walks with the wise will be wise.   PROVERBS 13:20

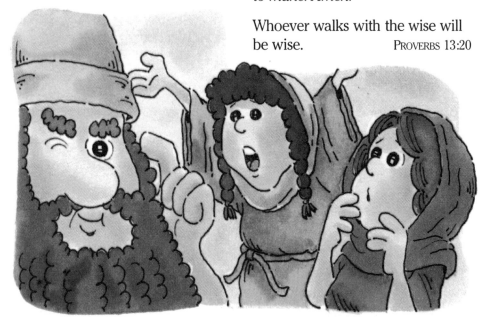

Daniel's Understanding

DANIEL 5

Daniel was in jail in Babylon. One night the king of Babylon was giving a party. Suddenly a hand appeared out of nowhere. It wrote a message on the wall. The king was so scared that he almost fainted. No one could understand the message. None of his wise men could tell the king what it meant. Then someone remembered the prisoner, Daniel. He was very wise.

Daniel told the king that God had sent the message. It was a warning that the king was going to be punished because he did not obey God.

When have you been able to explain something to a friend?

How did Daniel know what the dream meant?

Dear God,
I would like to be wise like Daniel. Help me spend time learning the Bible and talking to you, so I can be wise too. Amen.

If any of you needs wisdom, you should ask God and he will give it to you. God is generous to everyone and doesn't hold grudges. JAMES 1:5

107

Jamie Shows Wisdom

Jamie and Matt were playing in Jamie's back yard. Tommy, the new boy from down the street, was playing with them. The three boys played in the sandbox all morning. They built streets and tunnels and rolled their cars and trucks through each one.

When they were finished playing, they lay back on the grass and watched the clouds floating by. "I'm bored," Tommy said. "Let's do something exciting. Hey, I know, let's go in that garden over there and pull up some of those green things. I want to see what they look like underneath." Tommy got up and started to Mrs. Wilson's vegetable garden.

"Wait Tommy," Jamie called. "Mrs. Wilson works hard in her garden. It wouldn't be nice to ruin her plants. Let's play catch instead."

How did Jamie make a wise choice?

What wise choices have you made?

Dear God,
I have to make choices every day.
Help me make wise ones. Help me
to think about how you want me
to live and how my choices will
affect others. Amen.

Help me understand so that I may follow your teachings. I will guard them with all my heart.

PSALM 119:34

God Means What He Says

Sunday
"You Will Have a Child"

GENESIS 17:15-19; 21:1

When you have been told that something is going to happen, but it does not happen for a long time, how do you feel? Do you give up and think it will never happen?

That happened to Abraham and Sarah. They wanted a child. God told them they would have a baby. He said they would even have many many grandchildren, as many as there are stars in the sky.

But now Abraham and Sarah were very old and they still did not have even one child. They didn't think they would really have any children. They stopped believing God.

Then Sarah gave birth to a baby boy! Now Abraham and Sarah knew that God meant what he said.

How do you think Abraham and Sarah felt when the baby was born?

What have you had to wait for a long time to happen?

Dear God,
Waiting is so hard for me. Help me remember that when you say something, it is true. It will happen, just as you said. Amen.

God faithfully keeps his promises.
1 CORINTHIANS 1:9

"No More Big Floods"

GENESIS 9:12-17

When you see a rainbow, what do you think about? A rainbow means something very special.

One time God was unhappy with the way people were living. He was sad that no one tried to live for him. God sent a big flood that covered the whole earth. Everyone and everything died except a man named Noah, and his family.

Noah was the only one who tried to live for God. So God put Noah in a big boat and kept him safe during the flood.

When the flood was over, God told Noah to come out of the boat and live on the earth again. God promised Noah that he would never again send a flood so big that the whole earth was covered. As a sign of this promise God put a rainbow in the sky. Every time we see a rainbow, we can remember God's promise.

How do you think Noah felt when the flood was over?
What are some of God's other promises?

Dear God,
Thank you for beautiful rainbows that remind us of your promise. Thank you for always keeping your promises. Amen.

Whenever I form clouds over the earth, a rainbow will appear in the clouds. Then I will remember my promise to you and every living animal. Never again will water become a flood to destroy all life.

GENESIS 9:14-15

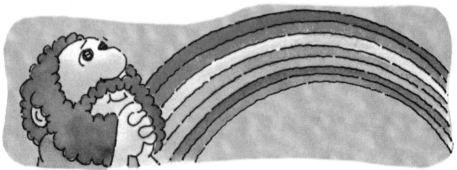

"You Will Have Bread and Meat"

Exodus 16:6-13

God cares about *every* problem we have. The Israelites were complaining because they were hungry. They got angry at Moses for taking them out of Egypt where they were slaves. All they cared about was the good food in Egypt.

God heard them complaining. He told Moses that he would send food for the Israelites. He would send bread every morning and meat every night. The people probably wondered how God would do this. They were in the middle of a desert. There was no food anywhere.

That night, birds flew in and covered the camp. The Israelites caught them for food. The next morning bread, called *manna,* came down from the sky. God meant what he said.

Did the Israelites trust God?

What can you trust God for today?

Dear God,
Thank you for caring about what I need every day. It is hard to be happy when I am hungry or tired. Thank you for taking care of me. Amen.

[God is] going to send you food from heaven like rain. Exodus 16:4

111

"You Will Live"

NUMBERS 21:4-9

Imagine if we could just look at a statue and be healed from a disease? That happened to the Israelites.

The Israelites were traveling through the wilderness when they started complaining. They complained because they had no homes, no food, no water. God was tired of their complaining. He had to show them again that he was with them. So God sent poisonous snakes to the Israelites' camp. Many people were bitten by the snakes. Some died and others were very sick.

Then God told Moses to make a bronze snake and put it on a pole high above the people. Anyone who looked at the bronze snake would be healed. Those people would not die from the snake bite.

Would you have believed that just looking at a little statue would make you well? Why did it work?

Dear God,
It must have taken a lot of faith for the Israelites to believe that just looking at the snake would heal them. When they were healed they saw that you mean what you say. Help me believe what you say too. Amen.

People looked at the bronze snake after they were bitten, and they lived.   NUMBERS 21:9

"You Can Have a King"

1 SAMUEL 8:6-22

Some people do not like to be different. They dress like their friends and act like their friends. The people of Israel decided they wanted their nation to be like all the other nations. They wanted a king to lead them, like everyone else had.

Israel was led by God's prophet, Samuel, now. When the leaders said they wanted a king, Samuel talked to God. God told Samuel to tell them how a king would take their sons to be in his army. He would make them pay taxes. But they didn't care. They still wanted a king.

God knew that a king was not best for Israel. But he let Israel have what they asked for.

Did Israel make a wise request?

Why did Israel want a king?

Dear God,
Sometimes you give us what we ask for, so we can learn that we didn't really want it. Please give me what you know is best for me. Amen.

The LORD told him, "Listen to them and give them a king."

1 SAMUEL 8:22

113

"You Will Win"

JUDGES 6:11-23

Some people will not believe things until they see proof. Gideon was like that. God's angel came to talk to Gideon. He said "The Lord wants you to save the Israelites." Gideon wasn't so sure about this. He was from the poorest family. Who would follow him? So Gideon asked for some proof that God would help him.

Gideon put some meat, bread and gravy on a rock. Suddenly God sent fire that burned up all the food. That was the proof Gideon needed. Now he believed that God would help him.

Why did Gideon need proof that God would help him?

Can you think of a time when you wanted proof that something was true?

Dear God,
Thank you for being patient when your children sometimes need proof from you. Help me to be strong enough to believe what you tell me. Amen.

The Messenger of the LORD appeared to Gideon and said, "The LORD is with you, brave man."

JUDGES 6:12

Grandpa's Bible

When Jamie came into the living room Grandpa was sitting on the couch. He was reading his Bible. Jamie sat down on the couch next to Grandpa. He wanted to ask Grandpa to play catch, but he would wait until Grandpa was through reading.

As Grandpa turned a page, a piece of paper floated out. Jamie picked it up. "What does this say?" Jamie asked. Grandpa read it to him:

"God said it.
I believe it.
That settles it."

"What does that mean?" Jamie asked.

"It means that I believe what the Bible tells us God said. No questions, no doubts," Grandpa answered.

How do you know Jamie's Grandpa loves God?
What can Jamie learn from Grandpa?

Dear God,
Thank you that I can trust your word. Thank you for the Bible that tells me what I need to know.
Amen.

Blessed is the person who places his confidence in the LORD.

PSALM 40:4

115

God Talks to His People

Joseph's Dreams

GENESIS 37:5-10

People in the Old Testament sometimes heard God speaking to them in their sleep. God spoke in different ways to different people. He spoke to Joseph in a dream.

God told Joseph things that were going to happen to him in the future. He told Joseph that there was important work for Joseph to do. Joseph was glad to know about the future. He was happy to serve God.

How does God talk to you? What important work can you do for God?

Dear God,
One way you talk to me is in my thoughts. Help me keep my mind filled with good thoughts so I can hear your voice. Amen.

Keep your thoughts on whatever is right or deserves praise: things that are true, honorable, fair, pure, acceptable, or commendable.

PHILIPPIANS 4:8

A Voice in the Night

1 SAMUEL 3

When you are sleeping very soundly and something wakes you up, it is hard at first to know what it was that awakened you.

Samuel was a young boy who worked in the temple. When he went to bed at night, he was very tired. One night Samuel was sleeping, when something woke him up. Samuel hurried to the priest he worked for. He thought the man had called him. Samuel asked him what he wanted. But that man had not called Samuel. This happened three times. Then Samuel realized that it was God who was waking him up. God wanted to tell Samuel something. He had a special message for Samuel.

How do you think Samuel felt when he knew it was God calling him?

How would you feel if God spoke aloud to you?

Dear God,
I know you do not usually speak aloud to your children anymore. But I can still know your words by reading the Bible and praying to you. Help me listen to your words and learn from them. Amen.

Then God's peace, which goes beyond anything we can imagine, will guard your thoughts and emotions through Christ Jesus.

PHILIPPIANS 4:7

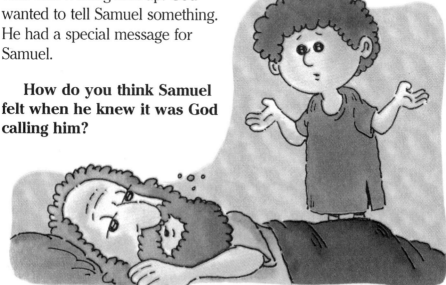

Tuesday

Nebuchadnezzar's Nightmare

DANIEL 2

Sometimes God has special messages for people who are not obeying him. He wants them to know what is going to happen to them. The special message may make them start to obey God.

God had a message for Nebuchadnezzar, the king of Babylon. One night Nebuchadnezzar had a dream. He did not know what it meant. None of his wise men or advisors could explain it to him either.

Nebuchadnezzar called for Daniel. He knew that Daniel obeyed God and God would explain the dream to him. God told Daniel that the dream was about the future of the kingdom. Nebuchadnezzar was happy to know what his dream meant and he knew that Daniel's God was very powerful. He made Daniel a ruler in the country.

Why would God have a message for someone who did not obey him?

Would you obey God if he gave you a special message?

Dear God,
I think anyone who had a message from you would want to obey. Help me to obey you every day. Amen.

Open your ears, and come to me! Listen so that you may live!

ISAIAH 55:3

Three Visitors

GENESIS 18:1-15

Abraham loved God. He obeyed God. God had a special message to give Abraham. He could talk to Abraham in a dream as he had some other people. He could speak aloud to Abraham. But he did not talk to Abraham either of those ways.

God sent three messengers to talk to Abraham. They looked like men, but they were angels. They came to Abraham's house. They ate with him and talked with him. The special message they had from God was that Abraham and his wife, Sarah, would soon have a baby boy. Abraham and Sarah were very happy.

What are some ways God talks to us today?

How would you feel if you knew you were talking to angels?

Dear God,
Thank you for good news. The good things that happen make me happy. They make the hard things easier to take. Amen.

Come close to God, and he will come close to you.   JAMES 4:8

Jacob's Dream

GENESIS 28:10-22

Jacob stole something from his brother Esau. Esau was very angry. Jacob was afraid Esau would hurt him, so he ran away from home.

Jacob walked a long way. He was very tired. When night came he laid down to sleep. He used a rock for a pillow. When Jacob fell asleep he had a dream. God told him everything was going to be alright, even though he had left his home. God told Jacob he would be with him and watch over him.

How do you think Jacob felt after this dream?

When have you wanted God to tell you that everything would be all right?

Dear God,
I am glad that you are always with me. Thank you for stories in the Bible like this one. I feel better knowing that you know what is happening to your children. Amen.

I am with you and will watch over you wherever you go. GENESIS 28:15

The Burning Bush

EXODUS 3:1-10

God talked to Moses in a different way. He had a message for Moses and he wanted to be sure Moses paid attention.

Moses was out in a field taking care of his sheep. He looked up and saw a bush that was burning. Moses went closer to see what was happening. The bush burned and burned, but it did not burn up. Suddenly, God called to Moses from inside the bush. God said that he had a job for Moses to do. He knew it would be a hard job, but Moses knew God would help him.

How do you think Moses felt when he saw the burning bush?

If God asked you to do something, what would you say?

Dear God,
You know how to talk to each of us. Some of us need a burning bush, some of us just need a Bible. Thank you for talking to us in the way that is best for each of us. Amen.

Those who love me will obey what I say. JOHN 14:23

Jamie Learns about Talking to God

"Mom, I wish God would talk to me like he did those people in the Bible," Jamie said.

Mom tucked the blankets in tight and said, "Yes, there are times when it would be nice to hear God's voice or know for sure what he wants us to know. But, we can always talk to God by praying to him. He talks to us through the Bible. That is why we should spend time reading it. It is his words to us."

"Is there any other way that God talks to us?" Jamie asked.

"When we are trying to live the way he wants us to, and we pray and read the Bible every day. Then sometimes he speaks to us in a quiet voice inside our heads," Mom answered.

"I guess that is a good reason to say my prayers right now," Jamie said.

When do you talk to God? Has God ever talked to you? When?

Dear God,
I want to live so that I am close to you. Then if you want to talk to me, I will be able to listen. Thank you for the Bible that talks to me any time I read it. Amen.

Pray in the Spirit in every situation. Use every kind of prayer and request there is. For the same reason be alert.

EPHESIANS 6:18

God Is the Great Comforter

Sunday

A Crying Mother

GENESIS 21:8-21

Ishmael and his mother, Hagar, were sent away from their home. Now they were in the desert with no food and no water. Hagar put Ishmael down under a bush. She went off a little way from him. *I just cannot watch him die*, she thought as she began to cry.

God heard Hagar and Ishmael crying. He sent his angel to talk to Hagar. The angel told Hagar not to be afraid. The angel said God would take care of her and her son. When Hagar opened her eyes, she saw that God had made a well full of water. So she got a drink for herself and her son.

How do you know that God cared when Hagar and Ishmael were afraid?

How do you think they felt after the angel talked to them?

Dear God,
You knew what was happening to Hagar and Ishmael, even when they were out in a desert. Thank you that you know everything that happens to me. Thank you that you care. Amen.

Let your mercy comfort me as you promised.

PSALM 119:76

123

A Sad Mother

2 KINGS 4:8-37

Does God care when his people are sad or lonely?

Once there was a woman in the town of Shunem who was very sad. Her only son had died and she missed him very much. The lady knew God's prophet, Elisha. When he was in Shunem he stayed in her home. So the sad mother went to find Elisha. She told him about her son. Elisha knew that God cared about the mother's sorrow. He went home with her and laid down on top of the dead boy.

Soon the boy's body was warm. Suddenly, the boy sneezed seven times, then opened his eyes. He was alive! God gave the boy back to his mother.

How do you think that sad mother felt now?

How does God show you that he cares when you're sad or lonely?

Dear God,
I know you don't always bring our dead loved ones back to life. But you always care about how we feel. Thank you for caring when I am sad or lonely. Amen.

He certainly has taken upon himself our suffering and carried our sorrows.   ISAIAH 53:4

A Man Loses Everything

JOB

When bad things happen to someone that does not mean God is angry with them. Sometimes bad things just happen.

Job loved God very much. But bad things happened to Job. His children died, he lost all his money, then he got sick too. But Job never stopped trusting and loving God. Did God care about all the bad things that were happening to Job?

Yes, God did care. He knew that Job really loved him. He gave Job more children, more money than before, and his good health back.

Why didn't Job get angry at God when the bad things happened?

How do you feel when bad things happen?

Dear God,
Some things are hard to understand. It's good to know that you care about how I feel. Thank you for taking care of me. Amen.

Praise the God and Father of our Lord Jesus Christ! He is the Father who is compassionate and the God who gives comfort. He comforts us whenever we suffer.

2 CORINTHIANS 1:3-4

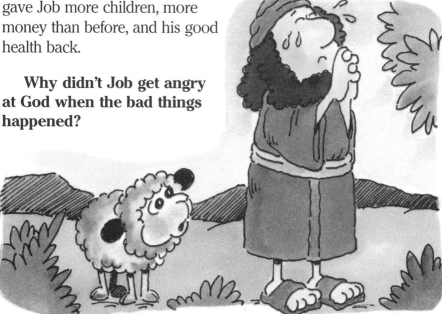

Wednesday

A Sick Man Is Healed

2 Kings 5:1-15

When people are very sick, they may wonder if God still cares about them. One time a man was sick with a terrible disease. His name was Naaman. He was a commander in the army. Naaman had a disease called leprosy. People who had leprosy had to go live together. They were not allowed around well people.

A young slave girl who worked for Naaman loved God. She knew God could heal Naaman's leprosy. So she told him to go see Elisha, a prophet of God. God could use him to heal Naaman. God did help Elisha and Naaman was healed!

Why did the young girl think God would help?

Are you surprised that Naaman listened to a little girl?

Dear God,
Thank you that sometimes people are healed of their diseases. Thank you that you always care about the problems we have. Amen.

Don't be afraid, because I am with you. Isaiah 41:10

A Sick King

2 KINGS 20:1-11

Did you ever wonder if God listens to your prayers? He listened to King Hezekiah. King Hezekiah was very sick. Isaiah, a prophet of God went to see him. He told the king, "God says you are going to die, so get ready." King Hezekiah started crying. He said, "O God, remember I have always tried to obey you!" King Hezekiah did not want to die.

God told Isaiah to go back to the king and say, "God has seen how sad you are. He will heal you!"

How do you think King Hezekiah felt after Isaiah said he would get well?

What are you sad about that you want God's help with?

Dear God,
Thank you for listening to my prayers. Thank you for caring how I feel about things. I am glad I can talk to you about anything. Amen.

This is what the LORD God of your ancestor David says: "I've heard your prayer. I've seen your tears. Now I'm going to heal you."

2 KINGS 20:5

Elijah Is Sad

1 Kings 19:1-18

But God knew that Elijah just needed some comfort. He sent an angel to give Elijah food and water. Then God told Elijah that he was not the only man left who loved God. He was not alone.

Do you think Elijah felt better after he ate and talked to God?

Are you sad about anything? Can you talk to God about it?

Dear God,
Sometimes we all need to feel better. Thank you for knowing that and helping us feel better. Amen.

Elijah was sad and afraid. The king was angry at him and wanted to kill him. So Elijah ran away. He went into the wilderness and sat down under a tree. Elijah was so tired of all his problems, he even thought he was the only man left in the world who loved God. "I am tired of all this. Just let me die," he begged God. Then he fell asleep.

I leave you with peace. I give you my very own peace. John 14:27

Jamie's Dog Dies

Jamie closed the door and laid down on his bed. He didn't feel so good. That afternoon, Jamie's dog, Pinto, had died. Pinto had been part of the family as long as Jamie could remember. He was going to miss him.

There was a soft knock on the door. "It's Mom, Jamie, can I come in?"

"If you want to," Jamie mumbled.

Mom came in and sat down next to Jamie. "I know you are sad," she said, "I am too. It's OK to cry, you know. It might help you feel better."

"Mom, I just don't understand why Pinto had to die. It really hurts. Doesn't God care that I loved Pinto? Doesn't he care that I feel bad?" Jamie asked.

"Of course God cares, Jamie. Remember the Bible stories of how he comforted sad people? Let's talk to him right now."

What do you think Jamie said to God?

Is there anything you need comfort for?

Dear God,
We all feel bad sometimes. Thank you for caring that we do. Thank you for making us feel better.
Amen.

Give God all your anxieties because he cares for you.

1 PETER 5:7

129

Becoming a Follower of God

Everyone Sins

ROMANS 3:23

Some people feel that they never do anything wrong. They think that sin is only big things such as killing another person or robbing a bank.

But the Bible tells us sin is anything that goes against what God says to do. You may try very hard to do the right things, but no one is perfect. Everyone sins. No one is as good as God. Sin is being selfish or getting angry. Sin is anything we do that makes God sad.

Name some things you know are sin.

What can you do to stop sinning?

Dear God,
I don't like to think about the things I do that are sin. But I am sorry for them. Help me stop doing wrong things. Help me live the way you want me to.
Amen.

I don't realize what I'm doing. I don't do what I want to do. Instead, I do what I hate.

ROMANS 7:15

Death vs. Life

ROMANS 6:23

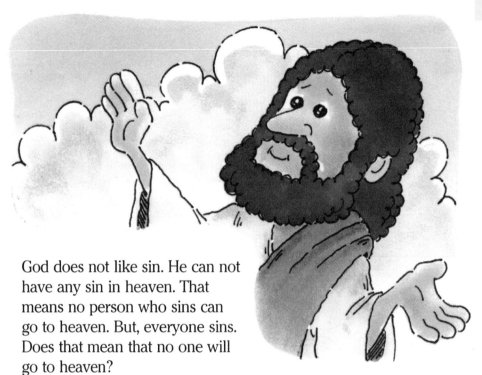

God does not like sin. He can not have any sin in heaven. That means no person who sins can go to heaven. But, everyone sins. Does that mean that no one will go to heaven?

God made a plan that helps people come to heaven. We can go to heaven because Jesus, the Son of God, came to earth. He lived as a person like us. He was hurt and died for us.

We can decide to believe in Jesus and have life. Or we can decide not to believe in Jesus and die. That means never going to heaven.

Why doesn't God want sin in heaven?
What is your choice?

Dear God,
I want to be able to live in heaven with you someday. Thank you for sending Jesus to earth. Thank you that he died for my sins. Amen.

The reward of the righteous is life. The harvest of the wicked is sin. PROVERBS 10:16

God Loved the World

JOHN 3:16

God loves everyone. He wants everyone to be able to live in heaven with him someday. He made a way for each of us to have a chance to come to heaven. God showed how much he loves us by sending his son, Jesus, to earth. Jesus came to die for our sins.

Some people that Jesus wanted to save were mean to him. But Jesus was willing to come. He was willing to go through everything that

happened. He did it because he knew it was the only way we would be able to come to heaven someday.

How does it make you feel to know God loves you? What would you like to say to him right now?

Dear God,
I love you too. Thank you for making a way for me to come to heaven. Thank you for sending Jesus to be the important part of that plan.
Amen.

Christ died for us while we were still sinners. This demonstrates God's love for us. ROMANS 5:8

Believe

JOHN 14:6

You know that everyone does wrong things. You have heard that no person who does wrong things can come into God's heaven. You also know that God made a plan so that we would be able to come to heaven. Now what?

The first step in becoming a Christian is to believe that Jesus is the Son of God and that he died for your sins. That is the only way to heaven. It is like a room that only has one door. The only way to get into the room is to go through that one door. Believing that Jesus is the Son of God and that he died for your sins is the doorway to heaven.

Do you believe that Jesus is the Son of God and that he died for you?
Will you tell him that?

Dear God,
I believe that Jesus is your son. I believe that he came to earth and lived as a person like me. I also believe that he died for my sins, even though he had never done anything wrong.
Amen.

I am the way and the truth and the life. No one comes to the Father except through me.   JOHN 14:6

Confess

1 JOHN 1:9

God is perfect and holy. He loves you and made a way for you to be able to live in heaven. He even calls you his children. How do you start down the path that will lead you to heaven?

The first step is to believe that Jesus is God's son and that he died for your sins. The next step is to understand that you have done wrong things. You must confess your sins to him. That means to tell him you know you have done wrong things. Tell him that you are sorry for those things. When you do this, he will forgive your sins.

Have you told God that you are sorry for the wrong things you have done?
Would you like to do that right now?

Dear God,
I do wrong things every day.
Sometimes I know they are wrong, and sometimes I don't.
But I am sorry for them. Please forgive me. Amen.

God is faithful and reliable. When we confess our sins, he forgives them and cleanses us from everything we've done wrong.

1 JOHN 1:9

Repent

Acts 3:19

If you were traveling down a road and discovered that you were going the wrong way, you would turn around and go the other way. That is what repent means.

When you are living without trying to please God, you do things that are wrong. That is sin. Then when you believe that Jesus is the Son of God and that he died for your sins, you want to change and live for him. That means you change the way you are living, you "turn around and go the other way." When you repent of your sins, God will forgive your sins and help you live for him.

Have you asked God to help you change the way you are living?

Can you change without his help?

Dear God,
I want to live the way you want me to. Help me change and stop doing things that make you sad. Thank you for forgiving my sin. Amen.

So change the way you think and act, and turn to God to have your sins removed.   Acts 3:19

Jamie's Decision

"Mom, can I ask you a question?" Jamie asked.

"Sure, what do you want to know?" Mom answered.

"Well, I'm just a kid. Can I ask Jesus into my heart, or is that something only grown-ups can do?"

"Jamie, I am very glad you asked that. Anyone can ask Jesus to come into his heart. Do you believe that Jesus is God's son?" Jamie nodded yes. "Do you know that you are a sinner and that Jesus died for your sins?" Jamie nodded. "And do you want to confess your sins?"

"Yes, Mom, I understand everything," Jamie said.

"Wonderful, then let's talk to God."

What is God's plan for us to get to heaven?

Do you believe that God sent Jesus?

Dear God,
I confess to you that I do wrong things, even when I don't mean to. Please forgive me and help me stop. Let Jesus come live in my heart and help me live the way you want me to. Amen.

God our Father loved us and by his kindness gave us everlasting encouragement and good hope. Together with our Lord Jesus Christ.

1 TIMOTHY 1:15

Psalms of Good vs. Bad

Psalm 1

Do you like to sing? Music is an important part of praising God. The Book of Psalms in the Bible are songs. They are some of the hymns of praise that God's people sang to him in Bible times.

The first psalm tells the difference between a person who wants to live the way God teaches is right and a person who does not. The person who lives for God will be blessed. But the one who gets advice from people who do not care about God, and who tries to be like them, will be punished someday.

What songs about God do you know?

What does *blessed* mean?

Dear God,
Thank you for the Bible. Thank you that I can learn how you want me to live by learning the Bible. Amen.

Blessed is the person . . . who delights in the teachings of the LORD.

PSALM 1:1-2

Psalm 36

If a man does bad things all the time, he soon stops thinking about God at all. He doesn't remember how powerful God is. He doesn't try to please God by the way he lives. He thinks he can be a good person all by himself. His whole life begins to show the wickedness in his heart.

But the person who loves God is surrounded by God's love and protection. There is no limit to God's love. God gives more blessings and joy than anyone can imagine. God is important in this person's life every day. The person who loves God knows God is caring for him constantly.

Would you rather be a person who loves God, or does not love God?

When have you felt God's love?

Dear God,
I love you. I am glad you are important in my life. Thank you for taking care of me. Amen.

Your mercy is so precious, O God. PSALM 36:7

Psalm 37

Does it sometimes seem like the sinful people always win? When you look around, do you see people who do not love God but have wonderful lives with good things always happening to them? That doesn't seem fair. It should be God's people who are the richest and have the best lives, right?

Psalm 37 tells us not to worry about this. Someday the sinful people will get their punishment. Someday the people who love God will get their reward. Just trust God. He is in control.

Do you know a Christian who has a hard life?
Will bad people be punished now, or after they die?

Dear God,
I am glad that the bad guys will be punished someday. I am glad that they will have chances to accept Jesus as Savior before that happens. Thank you for loving all of us. Amen.

The victory for righteous people comes from the LORD. He is their fortress in times of trouble.

PSALM 37:39

Psalm 73

It is good to trust God with no doubting in your heart. There may be times when you look around and see unfairness in the world and begin to doubt God. You may even feel jealous of those who have a good life, but do not obey God. Remember to think about God and how he will judge these people someday. No one gets away with disobeying God forever. They will be punished for the way they live.

Stay close to God. Let him be your guide and your strength.

What things do you think are unfair to God's people?

How can you stay close to God?

*Dear God,
Help me to keep my attention on you. Help me not to think about how other people are doing or what is fair or unfair. Help me to stay as close to you as I can. Amen.*

My body and mind may waste away, but God remains the foundation of my life and my inheritance forever.

PSALM 73:26

Psalm 112

The man who fears God is blessed! His children will have good lives. His good deeds will always be remembered. He does not ever need to be afraid. God will help him with everything. He is kind and generous and is fair with everyone.

The man who loves God will not be upset when bad things happen. He is not frightened by bad news. He knows that God will take care of him whatever happens.

People who do not love God will watch this man and be angry. They will run away and hide because they know that what they hope for can never happen.

Does this mean that a person who loves God will have no problems? What does it mean?

Dear God,
Thank you for taking such good care of people who love you. The blessings of loving you cannot even be measured.
Amen.

Blessed is the person who fears the LORD and is happy to obey his commands.   PSALM 112:1

Friday

Psalm 119:1-8, 89-96

The person who loves God's Word lives a happy life. Doing God's will makes him happy. He stands firm for what is right. He does not try to bend the rules just to get along with people who do not love God. He follows God's rules every day. He has nothing to be ashamed of. God is happy with him.

God's word will last forever. It was here when time began and it is still here. It does not change, it has always been the same. God's faithfulness to his people is proven by his word.

What Bible verse can you say from memory?

Say the Bible verse for today.

Dear God,
I love your word. Thank you for having people write it all down. Thank you that I can memorize it and keep it in my heart.
Amen.

I have treasured your promise in my heart so that I may not sin against you.

PSALM 119:11

Jamie's Memory Verse

"Jamie, tomorrow is Sunday School. Have you learned your memory verse?" Mom asked.

"No, I'll do it later," Jamie said.

"Let's do it now. I'll help you," Mom suggested. "I have the paper here that lists all the verses for the month."

"OK. If I learn this last one, I get a big chocolate candy bar," said Jamie.

"Well, that's a nice treat, but that is not the only reason you should learn memory verses. When you put God's word in your heart, it is always with you. Then when you are playing with a friend, or having a problem, you will be able to remember verses that can help you.

Why do you learn Bible verses?

What verse do you know that can help when you are sad?

Dear God,
Thank you for speaking to me
through the Bible. Thank you
that there are verses that will
help, no matter how I am feeling.
Amen.

Your word is a lamp for my feet and a light for my path.

PSALM 119:105

143

Thank You Psalms

Psalm 18

Do you feel good when people say nice things about you? It is nice when someone says thank you too. It is good to say nice things about God. It is good to say thank you to God too. Some of the Psalms are songs of thanks and praise to God for the help he has given.

Psalm 18 praises God for being so strong:

God, you are like a fort that your people can hide in. You are a shield that protects them. You are always ready to help your people. You do miracles to protect your people and defeat their enemies. Praise you, God!

What can you praise God for?

When do you need God to protect you?

Dear God,
Thank you for being so strong.
Thank you for taking care of me and helping me when I need your strength. Praise you!
Amen.

God arms me with strength and makes my way perfect.

PSALM 18:32

144

Psalm 33

Listen everyone! Be so full of joy that you just have to praise the Lord. Play happy songs of praise to him on your instruments. Sing joyful praise to him!

Everyone stand in awe of God. Remember he just spoke the words and the world came to be! He ruins the plans of those who do not obey him. But his plans will stand forever.

No one is saved by a big army or by his own strength. Only God can deliver us from our fears and enemies. We can always be happy in the Lord. We can always trust him.

What song of praise can you sing to God?

Who can keep you safer than God?

Dear God,
Thank you for making the world.
Thank you for keeping me safe.
Thank you that I can always trust you. Thank you that you will never leave me! Amen.

We wait for the LORD. He is our help and our shield.

PSALM 33:20

Psalm 66

Shout with happiness to the Lord! Sing praises to his name! Tell God how great and powerful he is! His enemies shake in fear. The whole earth knows how powerful he is. He will rule forever!

Praise God because he has protected his people. He tested his people and gave them hard burdens to carry. But in the end, he brought them to a good place.

I will come to you, O God, I will sing your praises. I will keep my promises to you. I called out to you, and you answered me because there was no sin in my heart.

Praise God who did not turn away from me and did not hold back his love.

What happy words can you shout to the Lord?
Tell a Bible story that shows how powerful God is.

Dear God,
Thank you for always being there for me. Thank you for not turning away from me when I do wrong. Thank you that I can say I am sorry to you and stay close to you. Amen.

Shout happily to God, all the earth!

PSALM 66:1

Psalm 107

Thank you God for always being so good! You saved me from my enemies, and I will tell everyone how wonderful you are. Some people wandered in the wilderness, hungry and thirsty, and God brought them to safety.

Some were foolish and full of sinful ways. They cried to God for help, and he saved them. Let them sing their thanks to him.

He has power over the stormy oceans. He dries up rivers and makes deserts green and fruitful. He brings the hungry and homeless to them so they can live. He blesses them and gives them big families. Think about everything the Lord has done. Think about how loving God is!

What story tells how God protected his people?
What would you like to thank God for?

Dear God,
Thank you God for your protecting power. Thank you for your love that blesses me and surrounds me. Amen.

Give thanks to the LORD because he is good, because his mercy endures forever.

PSALM 107:1

147

Psalm 118

Thank you Lord, for being so good. Your love lasts forever. Take refuge in the Lord, instead of the mightiest of men. The Lord is my strength and he gives me victories. Sing songs of joy because he is good. When my enemies surround me, I call on the name of God and he helps me. When I was about to fall, God helped me. He is my strength and my song.

You are my God, and I thank you for all you do. I will praise you. Your love will last forever.

How do you feel the Lord's strength?

How can you praise God for his love?

Dear God,
Thank you for your love and strength. I will trust you and not anyone else. Thank you for always being my helper. Amen.

The LORD is my strength and my song. He is my Savior.

PSALM 118:14

Psalm 139

O God, you know everything about me. You know when I am quiet and when I am busy. You know what I am thinking. You even know what I am going to say before I do.

There is no place I can go where you are not with me. You knew me before I was even born. Thank you that I am so wonderfully made. You planned all my life before I was even born. Your thoughts are precious to me, O God, and they are so many. Thank you that you never leave me.

I hate your enemies. I want them to be gone.

Search my heart, O God. If there is anything that needs to be changed, show me and lead me down your path.

How does it feel to know that God knows everything about you?

If God searched your heart, would he find anything that needed to be changed?

Dear God,
I am so glad that you are in complete control. I am glad that you are always with me. Thank you for planning my life before I was even born.
Amen.

Examine me, O God, and know my mind. Test me, and know my thoughts.   PSALM 139:23

149

Saturday

Jamie Says "Thank You"

Jamie listened closely as the choir sang in church. They were singing a song of praise to God. Then he listened as the Scripture passage was read. It was a chapter from Psalms. Pastor Jones' sermon was about praising God, too. When the family got home from church, Jamie had a question. "Dad, will you help me write my own song that praises God?"

"I think that is a great idea," Dad replied. "What would you like to praise him for?"

Jamie thought for a minute. Then he said, "Well, for my great family, for helping Grandpa get well, and for our church."

What things would you praise God for?

Make up a song praising God for those things.

Dear God,
Thank you for my family, and for my church. Thank you that you take care of me every minute of my life.
Amen.

I will make music to praise you.
PSALM 138:1

150

Proverbs to Live By

Sunday

Choose Good Friends

PROVERBS 1:8-19

What kinds of friends do you have? Did you know that your friends can make a difference in what kind of person you are?

If you spend your time with friends who do bad things and do not obey God, you will soon be like them. You will get so used to doing the things they do, that soon you will not even notice that what you are doing makes God sad.

So, if someone like that calls you to come and join them, run the other way. Make a wise decision and choose to spend your time alone or with friends who live in a way that is pleasing to God. You will be choosing wisely.

Who are your friends? What do you and your friends like to do?

Dear God,
Help me to choose friends who
will help me be a better person.
Help me to run away from
friends who want me to do
wrong. Amen.

If sinners lure you, do not go along.   PROVERBS 1:10

151

Trust

PROVERBS 3: 5-6

Would you like to know a simple plan that promises success in life? It would be nice to know that if you just live by a certain plan, everything will turn out right.

God gave us a simple plan in Proverbs 3:5-6. These verses say to trust God completely. Don't think that you know better than God, or that you can make better decisions than he does. Make God the most important thing in your whole life. Make him number one in everything you do. When he knows that he is that important to you, he will guide you and make your life a success. The success is a reward for serving him.

What does it mean to "trust God"?

How do you show that you trust God?

Dear God,
Thank you for guiding my life. I am glad I can trust you completely. Amen.

Trust the LORD with all your heart and do not rely on your own understanding   PROVERBS 3:5

Right vs. Wrong

PROVERBS 4:10-27

Choose to live your life doing right and you will live a good life. A person who chooses to do bad things ends up spending his whole day doing bad things. He wants to cause trouble for other people; in fact, he can't rest until he does.

For a good person each new day is an exciting adventure. But the bad person has trouble all the time and does not know why.

Guard your heart and keep it pure, don't say bad words, and keep on the path that pleases God.

When have you had to choose between right and wrong?

Do you know anyone who likes to cause trouble for other people?

Dear God,
Thank you for these reminders to live in a way that pleases you. Help me to make good choices. Amen.

Guard your heart more than anything else, because the source of your life flows from it.

PROVERBS 4:23

Week 20

Don't Be Lazy

PROVERBS 6:6-11

When Mom or Dad wants you to do a job, do they have to ask you over and over?

Have you ever watched an ant crawling on the ground? If you watch for a while you will see that the ant is busy all the time. He works and works storing food to eat in the winter. There is no boss telling the ant what to do, he just does what he knows he should do.

When you sleep all the time, you are not planning for the future. When you avoid work, you are starting bad habits. Do not make Mom and Dad keep after you constantly.

Do you get right to work when Mom or Dad asks you to do something?

What kinds of jobs do you have to do?

Dear God,
I don't usually like to do my jobs right away. Help me respond quickly when I am given a job to do. Amen.

Lazy hands bring poverty, but hard-working hands bring riches.
PROVERBS 10:4

Mom and Dad's Love

PROVERBS 13:24; 22:6

Did you know that when Mom or Dad punish you, they are showing that they love you? It's true! Proverbs says that one way parents show their love for their children is by disciplining them.

A parent could allow a child to do anything the child wanted to do. But that would mean the parent didn't care about teaching the child how to live or how to treat other people.

When a child is taught the right way to live, he will remember it when he is grown up. Then he will know how to live the way God wants him to live, and how to teach his own children to please God.

How do you know that your parents love you?
What do you get punished for?

Dear God,
Being punished is no fun, but I am glad my parents love me. I am glad they teach me about you and how to live for you. Amen.

Train up a child in the way he should go, and even when he is old he will not turn away from it.
PROVERBS 22:6

Listen to Wisdom

PROVERBS 8:12-36

Wisdom and good judgment go together. God's wisdom is free to anyone who wants it. In fact, in Proverbs we are encouraged to follow God's wisdom. God's wisdom in your heart gives good advice, and helps you make good choices.

God's wisdom has always been here. It was here before the world was made. It helped make the oceans and the mountains. Wisdom helps us learn about God everyday, whether playing with friends, or at home with our families. The best thing you can have in life is wisdom. When you have it, you will have life and favor from God.

How can you learn more about God's wisdom?
What is an example of God's wisdom?

Dear God,
I can learn about your wisdom by learning the Bible. Thank you for the Bible. Amen.

Listen to discipline, and become wise. Do not leave my ways.

PROVERBS 8:33

Jamie's Job

"Jamie, will you please pick up your toys and put them away?" Mom asked.

"In a minute," Jamie said. But he stayed on his bed looking at his airplane book.

A few minutes later, Mom called, "Jamie, do you have those toys picked up yet?"

"In a minute," responded Jamie, as he turned another page.

A whole hour later Mom started walking to Jamie's room, calling, "Jamie, I'm coming to check on those toys." But Jamie didn't hear Mom coming, he was sound asleep.

What proverb should Jamie have learned?

What do you think Mom said when she saw Jamie sleeping, and the toys still all over the floor?

Dear God,
I know my Mom and Dad are happy when I do my jobs right away. I know you are happy too. Amen.

Whatever you do, do it wholeheartedly as though you were working for your real master and not merely for humans.　　COLOSSIANS 3:23

More Proverbs to Live By

Be Careful What You Say

PROVERBS 11:12-13

When people get angry, they sometimes say things that they do not really mean. They usually are sorry later for what they said. But friendships may be ended because mean words were said. Even if you tell your friend that you are sorry for the mean words, it may be hard for your friend to forget what you said.

There is another way friendships are hurt. That is when a friend tells you a secret, and you tell it to someone else. When a friend tells you a secret, keep it to yourself. Your friend will not be happy to find out you told his secret to someone else. He will know that he cannot trust you with more secrets.

How do you feel when a friend says mean things to you?

How would you feel if a friend told one of your secrets?

Dear God,
Help me be a good friend. Help me say only kind words. Help me keep any secrets my friends tell me. Amen.

Whoever gossips gives away secrets, but whoever is trustworthy in spirit can keep a secret.   PROVERBS 11:13

True Happiness

PROVERBS 15:16; 16:8

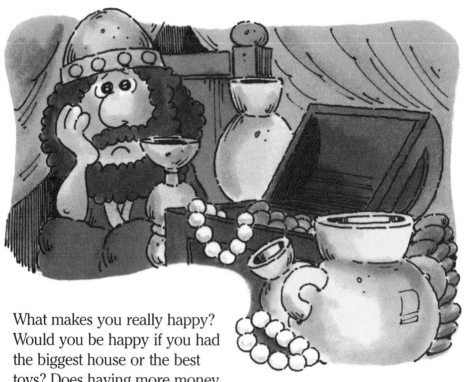

What makes you really happy? Would you be happy if you had the biggest house or the best toys? Does having more money than anyone else make a person happy?

A person may have all the money in the world. But he will not be happy if he does not know God. Serving God and living to please him is the only way to be happy. Otherwise you might look happy on the outside, but deep down inside, where only you and God can see, you are not happy.

What can you do to be happier?

Who do you know that always seems to be happy?

Dear God,
Thank you that I can be happy deep down inside if I live in a way that pleases you. Thank you that your way is best for me. Amen.

Better to have a little with the fear of the LORD than great treasure and turmoil with it.   PROVERBS 15:16

159

Constructive Criticism

PROVERBS 15:31-33

How do you feel when someone tells you that you are doing something the wrong way? Do you want to give up and let them do the job, or do you try to learn what they can teach you?

It is a good idea to learn when someone wants to teach you. If you turn down the help that is offered, then you will not learn the right or best way to do things. By following God we learn to be wise, and wise people want to learn as much as they can.

When has someone tried to help you learn the right

way to do something?
How did you act when they offered help?

Dear God,
It seems like I have a lot to learn all at once. Sometimes when I don't get things right the first time, I want to quit. Help me to not give up. I know everything I learn will make me a better person. Amen.

Give advice to a wise person, and he will become even wiser. Teach a righteous person, and he will learn more.   PROVERBS 9:9

A Good Reputation

PROVERBS 22:1

What does it mean to have a good reputation? It can mean that everyone knows you play fair; or that you are kind; or that you are not selfish. It could mean that your friends know that you do *not* play fair or do not try to be kind.

It is better to be thought of with kindness and love than to be rich or famous. The rich and the poor all look the same to God. What is in a person's heart is what makes the difference.

Who can you think of that has a good reputation? How do your friends think of you?

Dear God,
Help me to play fair and be kind
so that my friends, and most of
all you, will think kindly of
me. Amen.

A good name is more desirable than great wealth.   PROVERBS 22:1

How to Treat Friends

PROVERBS 25:17-20

Think about how you like your friends to treat you. Is that how you treat your friends?

Here are a few things to remember about being a good friend: Do not be at a friend's house every minute of the day; you will wear out your welcome, and your friend will not want to see you at all.

Do not tell lies about a friend that would make your friend feel like you beat her up.

Do not trust someone who can't be depended on, you will always get hurt.

If your friend is sad, do not try to cheer him up, that will only make him feel worse.

Which of these things can you do right away?
Which do you already do?

Dear God,
Help me be the kind of friend
that others want. Help me to live
so they will know that I love
you. Amen.

A friend always loves.

PROVERBS 17:17

A Good Wife and Mom

PROVERBS 31:10-31

Who washes your clothes, buys food for the family, cleans your house, and puts pretty pictures on the walls? Probably your mother.

Think about all the work your mom does to keep the family running smoothly. Dad may help, and you may help too, if you have chores to do. But Mom keeps things going.

She has kind words when you are sad, she kisses all your hurts. She gets up early to make breakfast for the family, she drives you where you need to go. Mom prays with you and reads Bible stories to you. Mom is an important part of the family.

Thank your mom for the things she does for your family.
Does your family have someone other than Mom who does these things? Who is it?

Dear God,
Thank you for moms and for dads too, who take care of us and keep our families going. Amen.

Her children and her husband stand up and bless her.

PROVERBS 31:28

Saturday

Jamie Learns A Better Way

Jamie and Dad were painting the fence around their backyard. When they finished, it would be a bright, clean white. Then Mom was going to plant some colorful flowers all along the fence. It would look great.

But the job for today was painting. Jamie grabbed a paintbrush and eagerly began slapping paint on the fence. He swished some paint from side to side, he swished some paint up and down. Soon Dad was at Jamie's side. He said, "Watch me, Jamie. This is how to paint." Dad carefully stroked the paintbrush up and down, up and down. "Make every stroke nice and even, and make them all in the same direction," he said.

"OK, Dad," Jamie said. He started over painting, up and down, up and down.

When have you learned the right way to do something by listening? Have you ever gotten angry because someone wanted to show you a better way? When?

Dear God,
It is always better to listen and learn from Mom or Dad. Help me learn from them, and from you too. Amen.

Those who take advice gain wisdom. PROVERBS 13:10

164

The Birth of Jesus

Sunday

Mary's Unusual Visitor

LUKE 1:26-38

Would you be willing to do anything for God? A young Jewish girl named Mary loved God. She would do anything to make God happy. God was very happy with Mary. He knew she loved him and wanted to serve him. God chose Mary to be the mother of his son, Jesus. He knew she would take good care of Jesus. God sent a special angel messenger to tell Mary the good news. She would be the mother of the Son of God.

How do you think Mary felt about the angel's news?
What did Mary do that made God choose her?

Dear God,
Thank you for sending Jesus. He was the most important part of your plan for us. Thank you that Mary was willing to serve you by being Jesus' mother. Amen.

Brothers and sisters, because of God's compassion toward us, I encourage you to offer your bodies as living sacrifices, dedicated to God and pleasing to him.

ROMANS 12:1

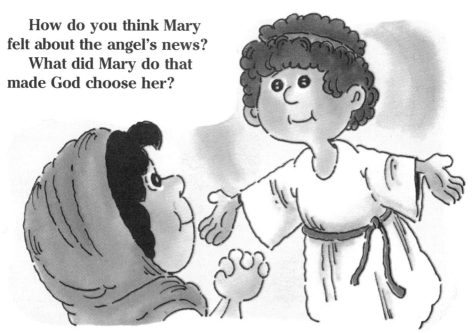

The Trip to Bethlehem

LUKE 2:1-5

The Old Testament Scriptures said that the Messiah [Son of God] would be born in the town of Bethlehem. Mary and Joseph lived in Nazareth. So how could Mary's baby be the Son of God?

That question was soon answered. The ruler of the land decided to count how many people lived in his land. But instead of just counting the people where they lived, he ordered everyone to go back to the cities where their grandparents had lived. That meant Mary and Joseph had to go to Bethlehem. It was almost time for the baby to be born. Everything was working out according to God's plan.

How did God know what the ruler would ask the people to do?

Do you think Mary and Joseph knew about the Old Testament stories?

Dear God,
I am glad you are always in control. Thank you that everything that happened to Mary and Joseph was in your plan. Everything that happens to me is in your plan too. Amen.

A child has been born for us. A son has been given to us.

ISAIAH 9:6

A Humble Birth

LUKE 2:6-7

Where would you think the Son of God would be born? In a palace or a castle, right? When Mary and Joseph got to Bethlehem, every hotel room was taken. There was not even a small room for them to rent.

The only place they could find to stay was in a stable. Jesus was born in a stable where animals lived. Mary wrapped her special baby in cloths and laid him in a manger. The Son of God was not born in a palace, not even in a church. He was born in a stable.

Where were you born? How do you think Mary felt when she laid the Son of God in a manger?

Dear God,
Jesus came for everyone, not just famous important people. I think that is why Jesus was born in a stable. Thank you for the gift of Jesus. Amen.

You will find an infant wrapped in strips of cloth and lying in a manger.

LUKE 2:12

167

Special Announcement

LUKE 2:8-18

The night that Jesus was born some shepherds were watching their sheep. They were sitting on a hillside outside the quiet little town of Bethlehem.

Suddenly the dark night was filled with light. The shepherds looked up and saw an angel in the sky. The angel said, "Do not be afraid. I have good news. Today in the town of David a Savior has been born. He is the Christ. This will be a sign to you: You will find a baby wrapped in cloths and lying in a manger." Then the sky was full of a whole choir of angels praising God.

When the angels were gone, the shepherds hurried to Bethlehem to see the baby.

How do you think the shepherds felt when the angels told them the good news?

How do you feel when you get happy news?

Dear God,
The shepherds must have been excited to see Baby Jesus. Thank you for telling them the good news. Amen.

Today your Savior, Christ the Lord, was born in David's city.

LUKE 2:11

168

A Bright Star

MATTHEW 2:1-12

Do you ever look at the night sky? There are thousands of stars in the sky. Have you seen a star that is much brighter than all the others?

After Jesus was born some wise men from another country came looking for him. They traveled very far to find Jesus. The wise men knew where to go because they saw a special star shining in the sky. The star moved through the sky and the wise men followed it. It led them to Bethlehem where young Jesus lived with Joseph and Mary. The wise men gave Jesus special gifts.

Why did the wise men give gifts to Jesus?

Why do we give gifts to each other on Christmas?

Dear God,
The wise men must have really wanted to see Jesus since they traveled so far. I would too. Thank you for the special star that led them to Jesus. Thank you for sending Jesus to earth. Amen.

They saw the child with his mother Mary. So they bowed down and worshiped him.

MATTHEW 2:11

Message For Joseph

MATTHEW 2:13-23

How do you feel when your plans are suddenly changed? Joseph's plans were changed. Joseph, Mary and Jesus were living in Bethlehem. One night Joseph had a special visitor. It was the angel of God. He had a message for Joseph.

The angel told Joseph that a bad king wanted to hurt little Jesus. God wanted Jesus to be safe. Joseph should take his family to Egypt so Jesus would be safe. Joseph did what the angel told him to do.

When was a time your plans were changed?
Why did Joseph do what the angel said to do?

Dear God,
I am glad that Joseph listened to the angel. He did a good job of taking care of Jesus. Help me remember that when my plans are changed, it might be because that is best for me. Amen.

You make the path of life known to me.   PSALM 16:11

Jamie's Favorite Day

"Christmas is my favorite day of the whole year. It's even better than my birthday!" Jamie exclaimed.

"Why do you like Christmas so much?" Mom asked.

"Because I get tons of presents. And 'cause Grandpa and Grandma come. And 'cause we have lots of food," Jamie listed his favorite things.

"Isn't there any other reason you like Christmas?" Mom asked. "Did you forget that Christmas is when we celebrate Jesus' birthday? Let's remember to thank God for his wonderful gift of Jesus this Christmas season."

Why do you like Christmas?

Name a Christmas song about Jesus.

Dear God,
Thank you for sending Jesus to earth. He is a special gift to us. Help me remember that Jesus, not presents, is the reason we have Christmas. Amen.

A virgin will become pregnant and give birth to a son, and she will name him Immanuel [God Is With Us].

ISAIAH 7:14

Jesus Was Human

Jesus Had Parents

LUKE 1:31; 2:33, 48

Is it ever confusing to think that Jesus is God's Son, but he was a person like you are too? What are some ways we can know that Jesus was a human being?

The Bible tells us that Jesus had parents like we do. An angel told a young girl named Mary that she would have a baby. The baby's name would be Jesus. Then the angel told Joseph about Mary's baby. Joseph and Mary were married. So Joseph helped take care of Jesus when he was growing up. God knew that Mary and Joseph would take good care of Jesus. They would help him learn many things.

How do you know that Jesus always obeyed his mom and dad?

Do you always obey your mom and dad?

Dear God,
Thank you for my mom and dad.
They take good care of me.
Thank you that Jesus had a
mom and dad too. That helps
him understand how I feel about
my parents. Amen.

Then [Jesus] returned with them [his parents] to Nazareth and was obedient to them.   LUKE 2:51

172

Jesus' Birth

LUKE 2:7

Were you born in a nice clean hospital with doctors to take care of you? God could have sent Jesus to earth in a flaming chariot pulled by angels, but he didn't. Jesus was born, like all other people on earth. But he wasn't born in a nice hospital. There were no doctors to help his mother, or care for him.

Mary and Joseph were in a small stable when Jesus was born. Mary wrapped her new baby in strips of cloth. There was no bed to lay him in. Just a manger, a place where the animal's food was kept. But, Jesus was born like all other people on earth. Maybe Mary wished she could lay her new baby in a soft bed. But she knew that God's plan was best.

How does a brand new baby look?

Look at a picture of you when you were a little baby. How did you look?

Dear God,
It must have been hard for you to send Jesus to be born as a baby. Thank you that he was. Since he was a person like me, he understands how I feel. Amen.

She gave birth to her firstborn son.

LUKE 2:7

173

Jesus Was Tempted

LUKE 4:1-13

One of the hardest things about trying to live for God is fighting temptation. Temptation is when you want to do something that you know is wrong. You may want to take a cookie. But Mom said not to have one before dinner.

Does Jesus know how it feels to be tempted? Yes, he was tempted by the devil. The devil promised wonderful things, if Jesus would worship him. The devil spent forty days tempting Jesus. That is longer than a month! Jesus knows what it feels like to be tempted. He knows how hard it is to say no. But Jesus did not give in to the devil's temptations. He always said no.

What kinds of things are you tempted to do?

What can you learn from Jesus about being tempted?

Dear God,
If Jesus could say no to the devil for forty days, I can say no to the things that tempt me too. Thank you for putting the story of Jesus' temptations in the Bible. It helps me be stronger. Amen.

Our chief priest is able to understand our weaknesses. He was tempted in every way that we are, but he did not sin.

HEBREWS 4:15

Jesus Had Friends

JOHN 11:5

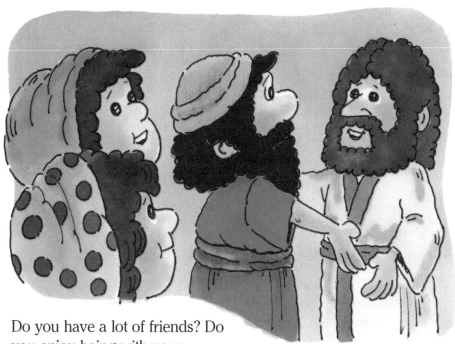

Do you have a lot of friends? Do you enjoy being with your friends? How do you feel when a friend is sick or moves away?

Jesus had friends too. Three of his friends were Mary, Martha, and Lazarus. They were two sisters and their brother. The Bible says that Jesus loved them. They must have been very good friends. Jesus often stopped at their home in the town of Bethany. Sometimes he had dinner with them, or just talked to them. It is good to spend time with friends.

Who are your good friends?

Can you talk to Jesus like you talk to a friend?

Dear God,
It is hard to imagine talking to Jesus like I do to my friends. I'm glad Jesus had friends, though. That means he understands how important my friends are to me. Amen.

Jesus loved Martha, her sister and Lazarus. JOHN 11:5

175

Jesus Felt Sad

JOHN 11:33-38

Jesus could make storms stop. He could make blind people see and crippled people walk. Why would Jesus ever have to feel sad? He could change anything that made him sad.

One time Jesus was sad. His good friend Lazarus had died. Mary and Martha were sad. They loved their brother. They would miss him. Jesus felt sad for them, too. Do you know what Jesus did? He cried. Now we know that Jesus understands how we feel when someone we love hurts very bad or dies.

When have you felt sad? How does it help to know that Jesus felt sad, too?

Dear God,
Jesus must have been very sad. Thank you that he understands how I feel when I am sad. Thank you for caring when I hurt. Amen.

Jesus' eyes were filled with tears.
JOHN 11:35

Jesus Died

LUKE 23:44-49

Jesus is the Son of God. When it was time for him to leave earth and go back to heaven, he could have ridden in a chariot of fire. He could have called thousands of angels to come and carry him to heaven. He could have left earth in many different ways.

But he did not choose any of those ways. Jesus left earth by dying, like we do when our earthly lives are over. Jesus died when he was nailed to a cross. Since he died, he understands how we may feel when death is near.

Do you know anyone who has died?

Why did Jesus die like a human does?

Dear God,
Death is scary because it means leaving everyone I know. The good thing is that when I leave earth, I will come to heaven to be with you. Amen.

When Jesus had taken the vinegar, he said, "It is finished!" Then, he bowed his head and died.

JOHN 19:30

177

"It Hurts, Mom"

"Mom, why does Grandpa have to be so sick?" Jamie questioned. "I prayed and asked God to make him better, why doesn't he do it? God doesn't understand how it feels to love someone that is sick."

"Yes, he does, Jamie. Remember when Jesus cried because his good friend died? He understands our feelings, because he felt them himself. That's one reason Jesus came to earth as a person. Since He knows how we feel, we can ask him to help us get through hard times. Let's talk to him right now. And Jamie, it is alright to tell God how sad you feel about Grandpa. He understands."

What do you think Jamie said to God?

What would you like to say to God about how you feel when you are sad?

*Dear God,
I really feel bad when someone I love is sick. I want you to make sick people better right away. Thank you for understanding how I feel. Amen.*

Turn your burdens over to the LORD, and he will take care of you.

PSALM 55:22

Sunday

Blessed Are Those Who Mourn

MATTHEW 5:4

Jesus spent much of his time teaching people how to live and what the kingdom of God was like. Jesus wanted everyone to know that God loved them very much. He also taught what is really important in life.

One of Jesus' sermons began with some ways Jesus expects his friends to live. It also tells what we can expect from him.

Jesus said, "Blessed are those who mourn, for they shall be comforted." Are you are sorry for the things you do that make God sad? That is mourning. Jesus promised to comfort all who are sorry for their sins. In the same way that a dad comforts his child, God will comfort and forgive the mourner.

What things have you done that you are truly sorry for?

How does your Mom or Dad comfort you? Can you feel God's comfort too?

Dear God,
Thank you for forgiving me when I am sorry for the bad things I do. Thank you for loving me. Amen.

"Comfort my people! Comfort them!" says your God.

ISAIAH 40:1

Monday

Blessed Are the Meek

MATTHEW 5:5

Do you know someone who is pushy and loud? Someone who always wants to have his own way? That person is not meek. A meek person is gentle, not pushy. But a meek person has a quiet strength inside. He is strong when it comes to standing up for what is right, or standing up for God. A meek person does not question God's wisdom or argue with God's directions.

Jesus said that the whole world and everything in it will belong to the meek. Does that mean that gentle people will own everything? No, it means that a person who is sorry for his sins and is willing to let God guide his life will have everything he needs for a happy life.

Can you think of someone who is meek? Who is it?

Do you know someone who is pushy and wants to have his own way?

Dear God,
Help me to be a gentle person.
Other people will want to be
around me if I am gentle. And if I
am gentle and trusting you, then I
will please you, too. Amen.

Oppressed people will inherit the land and will enjoy unlimited peace.   PSALM 37:11

Blessed Are Those Who Hunger and Thirst

MATTHEW 5:6

Have you ever been very hungry or thirsty? How did it feel? Jesus said that the person who hungers and thirsts for righteousness will be satisfied.

Some people want to hold on to the things they have such as a fancy car or lots of money. They think those things will make them happy. But soon, they realize that deep inside, they are not really happy.

The person who wants more than anything else to live for Jesus is the one who will be really happy. When you are hungry and thirsty for righteousness, you will want to learn more and more about Jesus and how he wants you to live. That is the only way to be truly happy.

How can you learn more about Jesus?

Do you want to be truly happy?

Dear God,
Help me remember that the things I have should never be more important to me than you are. Help me learn more about the way you want me to live. Amen.

Jesus told them, "I am the bread of life. Whoever comes to me will never get hungry, and whoever believes in me will never get thirsty." JOHN 6:35

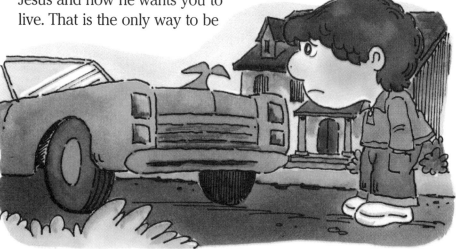

Wednesday

Blessed Are the Merciful

MATTHEW 5:7

If a friend does something mean to you do you want to hurt him as much as he hurt you? Do you wish you could get even? That would not make you feel better.

Jesus said to forgive others for anything they do. Trying to get even or holding a grudge will only make you feel worse.

God will forgive you for all the wrong you ever do. So you can forgive others for the wrongs they do to you. You can receive mercy by showing mercy.

When has a friend hurt you?

Have your forgiven your friend?

Dear God,
Help me be the kind of person
you want me to be. Help me to
forgive others and not hold
grudges. Amen.

Don't pay anyone with evil for the evil they did to you, or ridicule those who ridicule you. Do the opposite. Bless them, because you were called to inherit a blessing.

1 PETER 3:9

Blessed Are the Pure in Heart
MATTHEW 5:8

Jesus said that the heart is the most important part of your body. He was not talking about the heart inside you that beats and pumps blood through your veins. He was talking about what kind of person you are deep down inside.

Are you kind and fair and honest when no one is looking? You can pretend to be kind and fair, but what is in your heart will show through in everything you do and say. The real you cannot be hidden. You cannot change the kind of person you are by just changing clothes or hairstyles. You must go to God and ask him to change your heart. When your heart is clean and pure, you will see God.

Can a rotten apple be made clean by washing the outside?

How can you keep your heart pure?

Dear God,
Help me to have a clean heart so that others can see you in my life. Help me to have a clean heart so that I can see you. Amen.

Create in me a clean heart, O God, and renew a faithfult spirit within me.　　PSALM 51:10

Friday

Blessed Are the Peacemakers

MATTHEW 5:9

Pretend that two of your friends are fighting. They are shouting and crying, maybe even shoving a little. What do you do? If you are a peacemaker, you sit down with your friends and help them talk out their problems. You help them become friends with each other again.

Jesus said that the people in the world who are peacemakers will be called the sons of God. They know that it is more important to get along with others than to always be right, or always be the most important. What could be more wonderful than to be a child of God? Nothing in this world lasts forever, except being God's child.

When has someone been a peacemaker for you?
What does being a child of God mean to you?

Dear God,
Help me be a peacemaker. Help me remember that I do not always have to be right, or be first. Help me to put others first. I'm glad I'm a child of God. Amen.

The peace planted by peacemakers brings a harvest that has God's approval.

JAMES 3:18

Jamie Learns the System

Jamie was at it again—throwing a temper tantrum because he didn't get his way. He slammed the door and stomped around his room.

Soon Mom was knocking, "Can we talk?" she asked gently. Jamie grunted an angry "OK" and Mom came in. "Remember what we've been reading about Jesus' teachings in the Beatitudes?" she asked. Jamie stopped throwing books and looked at her. "The Beatitudes describe how God wants to make each of us more like him. Remember one is about what our hearts are like? I wonder if your heart is filled with selfishness and stubbornness right now. That is what is showing through. What can we do about it?"

What do you think Jamie did?

Do you need to talk to God about anything in your heart?

Dear God,
Thank you for the Bible that helps me learn how to be a better Christian. Help me to understand it and live the way you want me to. Amen.

I will find joy and be glad about you. I will make music to praise your name, O Most High.

PSALM 9:2

185

The Sermon on the Mount

You Are Salt

MATTHEW 5:13

Salt is sometimes used to preserve foods such as meats. A piece of meat is soaked in salt. That keeps it from spoiling. This was a common way of preserving meat before there were refrigerators or freezers.

Another use of salt is as a flavoring. If a little salt is sprinkled on food it is easy to taste. Salt makes plain food more exciting.

Jesus said that Christians are like salt in the world. People who do not know God will learn about him because they notice that Christians live differently.

Jesus said to be careful not to lose our saltiness. It is one way to help others know God.

Taste some salt right out of the salt shaker. What food has salt in it?

Has anyone helped you want to know God better?

Dear God,
Help me to be the saltiest
Christian ever. I want everyone to
know you! Amen.

You are the salt for the earth.

MATTHEW 5:13

You Are Light

MATTHEW 5:14-16

Have you ever ridden in a car late at night. Was everything outside the car window dark? Perhaps you could not see trees or sidewalks because there was no light. But way off in the distance you could see the lights of a city. When a light shines in the darkness, it is easy to see.

When you go into a room and turn on a light, you do not cover up that light. No, you let it shine so the room is full of light.

A person who loves God is a light in the darkness. He lives in a way that pleases God and that makes him a light that shows other people what God is like.

What different kinds of lights can you think of?

Who do you want to see your light and learn to love God?

Dear God,
Help me let my light shine so my friends will see it. Then I can tell them about you. I want everyone to love you. Amen.

I am the light of the world. Whoever follows me will have a life filled with light and will never live in the dark.   JOHN 8:12

Watch Your Anger

MATTHEW 5:21-26

If a person kills another person he will be punished. But did you know that you are not even supposed to get angry? Anger ruins friendships and even families. Anger makes people say things that hurt others. Maybe even call them names. Those are hurts that are hard to forget.

What if you want to tell God how much you love him, but then remember that a friend is angry with you. You should hurry to your friend and apologize to him. Then you can come back and tell God that you love him.

When someone is angry with you, get it settled quickly.

What makes you angry? Have you ever lost a friend because of an argument?

Dear God,
Friends and family members are so important. Help me to not say things in anger that would hurt them. Amen.

Everyone should be quick to listen, slow to speak and slow to get angry.   JAMES 1:19

Watch Your Language

MATTHEW 5:33-37

Do your best to be the kind of person who can be trusted. Do what you say you will do. Then when you make a promise to a friend you do not have to take a vow or swear that you will keep it.

Some people swear by the Lord's name that they will keep a promise. Jesus said not to do that. Others swear by heaven or earth. Jesus said to not even do that. When you make a promise just say, "Yes, I will" or "No, I won't." That's what God says to do.

How do you feel when you hear someone swear using God's name?

Can your friends trust you to keep your promises?

Dear God,
Please help me live so that my friends know they can trust me. Help me to keep my promises and mean what I say. Amen.

Do not take an oath on anything in heaven or on earth or take any other oath.   JAMES 5:12

Love Your Enemies

MATTHEW 5:43-48

Is there anyone you do not like or can't get along with? Do you know people who try to get you in trouble or talk you into doing things that you know you should not do. Those kinds of people could be called enemies.

Do you have friends? That would be people who like you and who like to do the same things you do. They are people who protect you and stick up for you.

Which of those kinds of people do you love? Just your enemies? Just your friends? Jesus said that anyone can love just their friends. It is harder to love your enemies too. People will see God's love in you if you can love your enemies as well as your friends.

Who do you have trouble loving?
Will you ask God to help you love that person?

Dear God,
I can love my friends—that is easy.
But I need your help to love some other people. Thank you for helping me with this. Amen.

Do for other people everything you want them to do for you.

LUKE 6:31

Be Generous

MATTHEW 6:1-4

Has your Sunday School class ever collected food or money to give to needy people? Many groups do this at Christmas time.

Jesus said that when we give to the needy or do other good deeds, we should do it secretly. Do not jump on the stage and shout that you are being generous or nice. Do your nice things without bragging and asking praise from other people. If you do your good deeds in front of others because you want them to tell you how wonderful you are, that is the only reward you will get. You will get no reward from God because you did good things for the wrong reasons.

What good deeds have you done?
Did you do them secretly or hoping that others would praise you?

Dear God,
Help me be a generous kind person. But help me be a secret good deed doer. Amen.

Be careful not to do your good works in public in order to attract attention. If you do, your Father in heaven will not reward you.   MATTHEW 6:1

Jamie's Offering

"Mom, Dad, LOOK!" Jamie shouted. He ran into the room carrying his beat-up old piggy bank. "Look, I have the last dime I need to make the bank open. Then I will have TEN WHOLE DOLLARS!"

"That's great son," Dad said. "What are you going to do with ten whole dollars?"

"I want to give it to the mission project in Sunday School," Jamie said. "Will you ask Mrs. Turner if she will announce it to the whole Sunday School? I want everyone to know that this is MY ten dollars! Then everyone will know how generous I am."

"Jamie, did you forget what Jesus said about doing our good deeds in secret? If you want the people in Sunday School to praise you for being generous, then that is your reward. You won't get a reward from God."

Would you rather have praise from people or God?
What good deeds can you do in secret?

Dear God,
Help me want to do nice things for the right reasons. Help me remember that pleasing you is more important than getting praise from people. Amen.

Give your contributions privately. Your Father sees what you do in private. He will reward you.
MATTHEW 6:4

Sunday

Do Not Worry

MATTHEW 6:25-34

When you get up in the morning, do you worry about what clothes you are going to wear? Do you worry about where you will get food for breakfast or lunch?

Jesus said that God takes care of every flower, even those that grow wild. If he takes such good care of flowers, that are here today and gone tomorrow, won't he take even better care of you? You can't change anything by worrying about it. So do not worry about how many things you own. Just try to please God, by how you live, then he will take care of everything you need.

What kinds of things do you worry about?
Will you trust God to take care of those things?

Dear God,
Thank you for taking care of everything I need. Thank you that I do not need to worry about anything. Amen

But first, be concerned about his kingdom and what has his approval. Then all these things will be provided for you.

MATTHEW 6:33

193

Do Not Judge Others

MATTHEW 7:1-6

When Mom or Dad reminds you to speak kindly to others, do you say, "They don't speak kindly to me!"

Jesus said that we should not criticize other people for doing things that we do too. We should not try to excuse our own behavior by pointing fingers at someone else. If you criticize others, they will not treat you kindly. They will treat you the same way you are treating them. It is best to take care of the problems in your own life before you criticize someone else.

When have you criticized others instead of correcting your behavior?

How can you be a good example to others?

Dear God,
Help me remember to let you be the judge of how others are living. Help me to be a good example for others. Amen.

You will be judged by the same standard you use to judge others.

MATTHEW 7:2

Ask, Seek, Knock

Matthew 7:7-12

If you ask your Mom for a piece of bread, does she give you a rock instead? Or if you ask for a fish, does she give you a snake? Of course not! Your parents would not give you anything that would hurt you. In the same way, God will only give you good things.

If God is an important part of your life and if you are living in the way that pleases God, you can ask him for anything. But make sure you are living for God, then the things you ask him will be what he wants to give you.

Why do you think God doesn't always give us what we pray for?

What good gifts has God given you?

Dear God,
Thank you for the good gifts you give me. Thank you that I can talk to you about what is important to me and know that you care. Amen.

If you live in me and what I say lives in you, ask for anything you want, and it will be done for you.

John 15:7

The Narrow Way

MATTHEW 7:13-14

When you walk down a hall that is narrow you have to be careful to walk straight or you will bump into the walls. There are two paths that you can choose from in life. The one that leads to heaven is a very narrow path. When you choose that way you must walk very straight. That means you live the way God tells you in the Bible.

Some people choose the path that does not lead to heaven. It is a very wide path. It looks like this path has more freedom and would be more fun. But since it does not lead to heaven, it only leads to unhappiness.

Which path are you on?

If you have not made a choice, ask your mom or dad to help you make the right choice.

Dear God,
Thank you that there are only two choices. It is easier to choose when I know I am deciding between right and wrong. Amen.

I can guarantee this truth: Those who listen to what I say and believe in the one who sent me will have eternal life. They . . . have already passed from death to life   JOHN 5:24

Be Fruitful

MATTHEW 7:15-23

Just because a person knows the words to say that make him sound like a Christian, does not mean he is a Christian. You can't fool God, he knows what is in your heart.

Jesus said you can tell if a person is really part of God's family by how he lives. A thorn bush does not grow grapes. A tree that grows tasty sweet fruit would not grow sour fruit that could not be eaten. In the same way, a person who is really living for God would not do bad things. Just saying Christian words is not enough, God must be part of a person's life.

What are "Christian words"?

Is God part of your life?

Dear God,
Please help me to be sincere. I do not want to pretend that you are part of my life, I want to know that you are. Amen.

Good people produce good things from the good stored in them.   LUKE 6:45

The Foolish Builder

MATTHEW 7:24-29

Jesus taught that a person who hears his teachings and uses them in his life is like the man who builds a house on a rock. The rock is solid and makes a good foundation. So the house stands firm in storms.

But the house that is built on sand does not have a good foundation. When storms come, it will fall down. That is like the person who does not have Jesus in his life. He does not have a good foundation. So when life gets hard, he will not have the strength to get through.

When you build something in sand, what happens to it when rain comes?

What happens to rocks when it rains?

Dear God,
Thank you for being solid and strong like a rock. I'm glad to know that you will help me get through whatever comes into my life. Amen.

Do what God's word says. Don't merely listen to it, or you will fool yourselves.   JAMES 1:22

Answer for Yourself

Jamie and Tommy played together all afternoon. Mom was in and out of the room. Everytime she came through, the boys were playing nicely. But late in the afternoon as she passed by the door, she heard Jamie shout, "You're mean! I don't want to be your friend anymore!"

"What's going on, guys?" Mom asked. Jamie and Tommy were on opposite sides of the room. Neither of them looked very happy. "Jamie, I think I heard you say something to your friend that was not very nice."

"But Mom, do you want to hear what Tommy said to me . . ." Jamie started.

"No, I don't," Mom interrupted. "Remember what Jesus taught us about the way to treat others? We each must be responsible for our own actions. We should not criticize others. Especially when they are just doing the same things we do."

Why did Jamie think it was OK to get angry at Tommy?

What does it mean to "be responsible for your own actions?"

Dear God,
Help me not to criticize others for the same things I do. Help me to be as patient with others as I want them to be with me. Amen.

Forgive and you will be forgiven.
LUKE 6:37

The Miracles of Jesus

Sunday

The Miracle Water

JOHN 2:1-11

Jesus did many miracles while he was on earth. People saw him do them and believed that he was the Son of God.

Jesus' first miracle was when Jesus and his friends were at a wedding. Jesus' mother was there also. In the middle of the wedding celebration, the host ran out of the wine which was being served to the guests. It would have been poor manners to stop serving the guests. So Jesus' mother came and asked him to help with the problem.

The servants brought six big jars to Jesus. He told them to fill the jars with water. Then he said,

"Now dip some out and take it to the host." When the host took a drink, it wasn't water anymore; it was wine! And it was even better than the wine they had been serving!

What was Jesus' miracle? Will Jesus help you with any problem you have?

Dear God,
Thank you for caring about any problem I have. Thank you that you can do miracles to help me. Amen.

Cana in Galilee was the place where Jesus began to perform miracles. He made his glory public there, and his disciples believed in him.

JOHN 2:11

The Quiet Storm

MATT. 8:23-27; MARK 4:35-41; LUKE 8:22-25

One time Jesus' disciples were afraid. They were on a boat crossing the Sea of Galilee. Jesus was with them, but he was asleep.

Suddenly a big storm came up. The wind began blowing very hard and their boat was being tossed around on the water. The disciples were afraid. They ran and woke Jesus. "Don't you care that we are going to die?" they asked.

Jesus stood up and looked at the water. "Be still!" he ordered. Instantly, the storm was gone. The sea was quiet and the wind stopped blowing.

This miracle showed his disciples that Jesus was in charge of everything, even the wind and the rain.

Who comforts you when a storm comes?

What other things make you afraid?

Dear God,
I'm glad you are in charge of
everything, even the weather.
Thank you for taking care of me
and helping me oe brave. Amen.

Even the wind and the sea obey Him.   MATTHEW 8:27

Lunch for 5,000

MATT. 14:15-21; MARK 6:35-44; LUKE 9:12-17;

News about Jesus spread quickly. People heard that he taught about God and that he would heal the sick. Crowds followed him everywhere he went.

One time Jesus got on a boat and went across the lake to rest. But the crowds of people hurried around the lake and waited for him. So he preached to them and healed the sick. It got late in the day, so some of the disciples said, "Send the people home so they can eat."

Jesus' answer surprised them. He said, "No. You feed them." They did not have any food or money to buy food for all the people. They searched the crowd and found a boy who had brought a lunch of five loaves of bread and two fish. The boy gave it to Jesus. He blessed the food and broke it into pieces. There was enough food for everyone! Over 5,000 people ate all they wanted and there were leftovers.

Why did the people follow Jesus everywhere?

What do you want Jesus to help you with?

Dear God,
This story shows me that you care about whether I'm hungry or cold or lonely. You will help me with those problems. I should do what I can to help people around me who are cold or hungry too.
Amen.

Then he took the five loaves and the two fish, looked up to heaven, and blessed the food. He broke the loaves apart and kept giving them to the disciples to give to the crowd.

LUKE 9:16

Walking on Water

MATT 14:22-27; MARK 6:47-51; JOHN 6:16-21

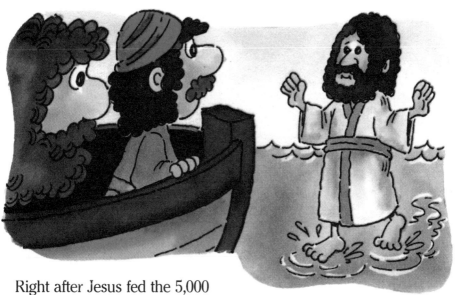

Right after Jesus fed the 5,000 people, he sent his disciples across the lake on boats.

Jesus went up on a hillside alone to pray. It was the middle of the night when Jesus went to join his friends. Their boat was out in the middle of the lake by now. But Jesus went to them anyway. He walked on top of the water. The disciples saw a man coming, but they did not know it was Jesus. They were afraid and cried out, "It's a ghost!"

Jesus heard them and he immediately said, "Be brave! Don't be afraid. It is I." Then he got in the boat with them. Now they knew he was the Son of God.

Why were the disciples afraid?

Did Jesus want them to be afraid?

Dear God,
Thank you for all the examples
that show Jesus is your son.
Thank you that I can trust you for
everything. Amen.

Jesus said, "Calm down! It's me. Don't be afraid!"

MATTHEW 14:27

Thursday

Fishing with Jesus

LUKE 5:4-11

Simon and his friends fished all night. But they did not catch any fish. Early in the morning they were back on shore cleaning their fishing nets. Jesus was close by, teaching some people. When he saw their boats he got in one and had Simon row out a little way from the shore. Then Jesus sat down and taught the people.

When he was finished teaching, Jesus said to Simon, "Put your fishing net down there in the deep water. You will catch a lot of fish."

Simon answered, "We've been fishing all night and have not caught even one fish. But since it is you who wants us to try again, we will." They let the nets down and when they tried to pull them up, the nets were so full of fish they nearly tore. Simon and his friends did not know what to think. Jesus said, "Don't be afraid; from now on you will catch men." So Simon and his friends left their boats and followed Jesus.

Why did Simon agree to try fishing again?

Why did Simon leave his fishing boat?

Dear God,
When I read what wonderful things you can do, then I know that the things I am able to do are just gifts from you. Thank you for them. Amen.

From now on you will catch people instead of fish.   LUKE 5:10

Lazarus Is Alive!

JOHN 11:1-44

Mary, Martha and Lazarus were good friends of Jesus. The two sisters and their brother lived in Bethany and Jesus often visited them.

One time Lazarus got very sick. His sisters sent for Jesus because they believed he could help their brother. Jesus was not very far away, but he did not come right away. By the time he came, Lazarus was dead. Everyone was very sad. Jesus was sad too.

But Jesus even has power over death. He went to Lazarus' tomb and called for the dead man to come out. Lazarus walked right out. He was alive!

Why did Mary & Martha think Jesus could help Lazarus?

Why was Jesus sad?

Dear God,
Death is a scary part of life. I'm glad to know that you have power over it too. Amen.

I am the one who brings people back to life, and I am life

JOHN 11:25

Jamie Is Afraid

Boom! Crash! Thunder was pounding across the sky. Flashes of lightning filled the room. Jamie had his head buried under his blanket and he was shouting, "Mom, Dad!"

"It's just a thunderstorm, Jamie. It's loud, but it won't hurt you," said Dad.

"I prayed for Jesus to stop it . . . like he did for the disciples. But, it just keeps going. Why doesn't he do a miracle for me?" Jamie asked.

"I don't know, Honey. Jesus does miracles when they will bring glory to God. But, he did send you a mom and dad who love you and will take care of you," Mom said as she snuggled Jamie on her lap.

What makes you afraid? What makes you feel better?

Dear God,
I'm glad for Mom and Dad who help me not be scared. And I'm glad I can talk to you. That helps me be brave too. Amen.

Trust the LORD.

PSALM 37:3

Sunday

Blind Bartimaeus

Mark 10:46-52

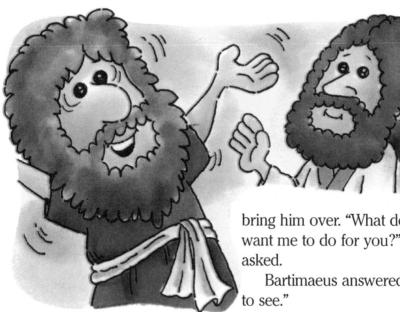

A large crowd of people was walking with Jesus and his disciples as they left the city of Jericho. A blind man named Bartimaeus was sitting near the road and he heard the crowd passing by. When Bartimaeus found out that it was Jesus the crowd was following, he began to shout: "Jesus, have mercy on me!" The people around him told Bartimaeus to be quiet, but he kept shouting.

Jesus heard Bartimaeus calling and told someone to bring him over. "What do you want me to do for you?" Jesus asked.

Bartimaeus answered, "I want to see."

Jesus said, "Go on your way. Your faith has healed you." Right then, Bartimaeus could see!

What problem did Bartimaeus have?

Who did he think could help him?

Dear God,
Thank you that Jesus healed Bartimaeus. Thank you that I can see all the wonderful things you have made for me. Amen.

Go, your faith has made you well.
Mark 10:52

207

The Deaf Mute

MARK 7:31-37

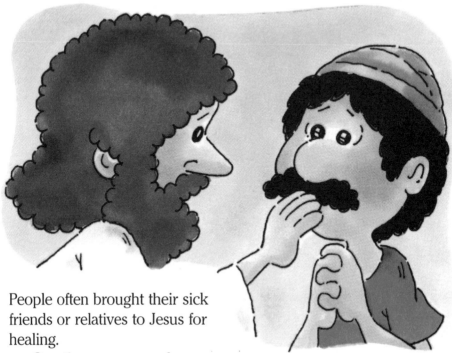

People often brought their sick friends or relatives to Jesus for healing.

One time some people brought a man who could not hear or speak to Jesus. They begged Jesus to heal him.

Jesus took the man away from the crowd. He put his fingers gently in the man's ears. Then he put some of his own saliva on his finger and touched the man's tongue. Jesus looked to heaven and prayed, "Be opened!" Suddenly the man could hear and he could speak clearly!

How could you help someone who is sick?

Who have you prayed for that needed healing?

Dear God,
Thank you that you can do anything. Thank you that if I have complete faith in you, miracles could happen for me. Amen.

If you believe, you will receive whatever you ask for in prayer.

MATTHEW 21:22

Jesus Heals a Woman with Great Faith

MATTHEW 9:20-22; MARK 5:25-29; LUKE 8:43-48

Jesus was in the middle of a crowd of people. They were pressing in close, just to get a glimpse of this man who did many miracles. Suddenly Jesus stopped and said, "Who touched me?"

His followers said, "Look how many people there are crowding around you. It is impossible to say who touched you." But then a woman came forward. She said she had been to many doctors for the last twelve years. None of them could help her with her health problems. But she believed that if she could just touch the bottom of Jesus' robe, she would be healed. The woman was afraid she was in trouble for touching him. But Jesus said, "Go in peace. Your faith has healed you." The woman was healed.

Why did the woman want to touch Jesus?

Was she healed because of her faith or because his robe was magic?

Dear God,
Help me to have faith as strong as the woman in this story. Help my faith to grow stronger every day. Amen.

What you have believed will be done for you.   MATTHEW 9:29

Ten Lepers

Luke 17:11-19

Leprosy is a terrible disease that rots away the skin. Jesus was on the way to Jerusalem when he met ten men who had leprosy. They begged him to heal them. Jesus said, "Go show yourself to the priests." So the ten lepers ran to find the priests. As they were running, they were healed of their leprosy.

When one of the men saw that he was healed, he turned around and ran back to Jesus. "Thank you for healing me!" he cried.

Jesus said, "Didn't I heal ten men? Where are the other nine? Only this one, who is from another country, came back to thank me?" Then he told the healed man to go home. His faith had made him well.

What has God done for you? Did you remember to thank him?

Do you think Jesus felt sad that the other nine did not say "thank You"?

Dear God,
Thank you for every wonderful thing you have given me. I am sure I do not say thank you as often as I should. Help me remember to be thankful and not just expect good things from you. Amen.

I will proclaim the name of the LORD. Give our God the greatness he deserves!

Deuteronomy 32:3

Jairus' Daughter

MATT. 9:23-25; MARK 5:22-42; LUKE 8:41-56

Most of the synagogue leaders did not believe that Jesus was the Son of God. But Jairus was a synagogue leader who did believe. Jairus' young daughter was very sick. In fact, he was afraid she was going to die. So Jairus went to see Jesus. He asked Jesus to come and touch his daughter. He knew Jesus could heal the little girl.

Jesus and Jairus were on their way to the girl when a messenger came to report that the girl had died. But Jesus said, "Don't be afraid, just believe." When they got to the house, people were standing around crying loudly. Jesus said, "Why are you making all this noise? The girl is not dead, she is just sleeping." Everyone laughed at him.

Jesus sent everyone out of the room except the parents of the little girl. Then he said, "Little girl, get up!" She did! She was alive again!

Why did people laugh at Jesus?

When you pray for someone's healing, do you believe Jesus will answer?

Dear God,
Jairus must have been very happy! Thank you that you can heal anyone you want to. Thank you for always knowing what is best. Amen.

Jesus went in, took her hand, and the girl came back to life.

MATTHEW 9:25

A Healed Servant

MATT. 8:5-13; LUKE 7:1-10

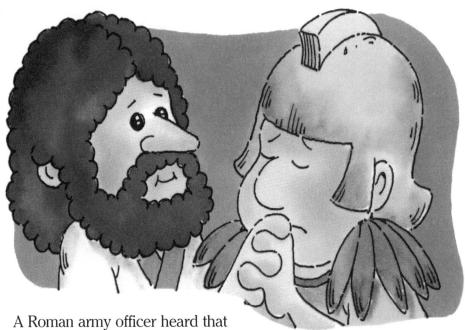

A Roman army officer heard that Jesus was in his town. He hurried to ask Jesus for his help. "My servant is very sick. He is in a lot of pain," he said.

"I will come to your house and see the sick man," Jesus said.

"Oh, I do not deserve to have you come to my house. If you just say the word, my servant will be healed," the Roman said. Jesus was amazed. He told his disciples that he had never seen anyone with so much faith.

"Go on home," he said. "Your servant is healed." At that very moment the servant was well.

If you could ask Jesus for anything, would you ask for something for yourself, or for a friend?

What amazed Jesus?

Dear God,
I would like to have the kind of faith the Roman officer had. Help my faith to grow. Amen.

No one can please God without faith.

HEBREWS 11:6

Jamie Wants a Miracle

" . . . and please help Grandma Warren to get well so she can go home real soon. Amen." Jamie climbed into bed and Mom tucked his covers in and kissed him good-night. "Mom, will God answer my prayer?" Jamie asked.

"He always answers our prayers," Mom said.

"So Grandma really will get well and go home from the hospital?" Jamie was so excited he was bouncing up and down.

"Well, I can't promise that," Mom began slowly.

"But that's what I prayed."

"I know," said Mom, "but Jesus doesn't always answer our prayers with yes. He doesn't always do miracles for us. We have to trust him to know what's best for us and for Grandma Warren."

What sick person have you prayed for?

What is a prayer God has answered for you?

Dear God,
Thank you for hearing my prayers. Thanks for all the special things you do for me. Amen.

That's why I tell you to have faith that you have already received whatever you pray for, and it will be yours.

MARK 11:24

213

Stories Jesus Told

The Sower

MATTHEW 13:1-23; MARK 4:3-20; LUKE 8:5-16

There was a man who was planting seeds. Some seed fell on the path and birds came and ate it. Some fell on rocky ground. Those seeds grew quickly, but they had no roots. Other seed fell in thorny bushes and were choked by them. Some seed fell on good ground and a good crop was grown.

Then Jesus explained what this story was really about. The seed on the path is a person who hears the Word of God but doesn't understand it. Satan comes and grabs it away from him. The seed on rocky ground is a person who hears the Word and receives it, but doesn't keep learning more about it. He doesn't have good roots so when trouble comes he gives up. The seed in thorny bushes is the person who accepts the Word, but lets the worries of life drown out the Word. The seed on good ground is the man who accepts God's Word and goes out and tells others.

Which kind of ground is the best for growing?
Have you accepted God's message of love?

Dear God,
Thank you for your Word. Thank you for your message of love. Thank you for helping me understand it. Amen.

I will put my teachings inside them, and I will write them on their hearts.

JEREMIAH 31:33

Story of the Weeds

MATTHEW 13:24-30, 36-43

Jesus said the kingdom of heaven is like a man who plants seeds that will grow good crops in his field. But while he is sleeping one night, his enemy comes and throws seeds that will grow weeds in the field. When the plants come up it is hard to tell which ones are good plants and which ones are weeds. So the farmer lets both plants grow until harvest time, then the weeds will be pulled out and burned.

Jesus explained that he was the one sowing the good seed. The field was the world and the good seed are the people who are part of God's family. The enemy is Satan and the weeds are his followers. The weeds are burned, just as Satan and his followers will someday be destroyed.

Ask an adult to show you the difference between a good plant and a weed.

Who do you know that needs to hear about Jesus?

Dear God,
Thank you that I am part of your family. I am glad to know that I will be in heaven with you someday. Amen.

Then the people who have God's approval will shine like the sun in their Father's kingdom.

MATTHEW 13:43

Tuesday

The Mustard Seed

MATT. 13:31-32; MARK 4:30-32; LUKE 13:18-19

Have you ever seen a mustard seed? It is a tiny seed. But the mustard plant grows so big that a bird can sit on it's branches.

Jesus said that a mustard seed is like the kingdom of God. His kingdom began very small, but many people joined the kingdom because they believed in Jesus. More and more are joining every day. Perhaps God's kingdom didn't look like much in the beginning when Jesus came to earth as a tiny baby. But someday God's kingdom will be the biggest and most important kingdom ever.

When have you planted a seed and watched the plant grow?

Who can you tell about God's kingdom?

Dear God,
Thank you that your kingdom keeps growing and growing. I am glad it will be the biggest kingdom ever. Amen.

Praise the LORD, my soul.

PSALM 104:35

The Lost Sheep

MATTHEW 18:12-14; LUKE 15:4-7

Did you know that every person is important to God? Jesus asked, "What if a man owned one hundred sheep and one of them got lost? Would he say, 'Well, I still have ninety-nine'?

"No," Jesus said, "he will leave the ninety-nine and go look for the lost one. When he finds it he will be happier about that sheep than he is about the others back at home."

Jesus said that in the same way there will be more happiness in heaven over one sinner who comes back to God than over 99 people who never turned away from him.

What have you lost that you looked for a long time?
How does it feel to know you are important to God?

Dear God,
It makes me feel very special to know I am important to you. I am glad that every person is important to you. Amen.

There will be more happiness in heaven over one person who changes the way he thinks and acts than over 99 people who already have God's approval.

LUKE 15:7

The Unmerciful Servant

MATTHEW 18:23-34

Peter asked Jesus, "How many times should I forgive someone? Seven times?"

Jesus said, "No, even more times. It is like a king who decided to collect the money one of his servants owed him. The man owed a large amount of money and he could not pay it. Since he couldn't pay, the king ordered the man and his family to be sold as slaves. The man begged the king for mercy. He promised to pay what he owed. The king felt bad, so he canceled the debt.

"Then that man went out and found a man who owed him a little bit of money. He choked him and demanded the money. Then he had the man thrown in jail. When the king found out, he was very angry. He said, 'I canceled your big debt. Shouldn't you have canceled his smaller debt?' Then the king put the first man in jail. That is what the heavenly Father will do if you do not forgive others."

When have you been forgiven for something?
When have you forgiven someone?

Dear God,
Thank you for your forgiveness.
Help me to be more forgiving of those around me. Amen.

Forgive us as we forgive others.
MATTHEW 6:12

Vineyard Workers

MATTHEW 20:1-16

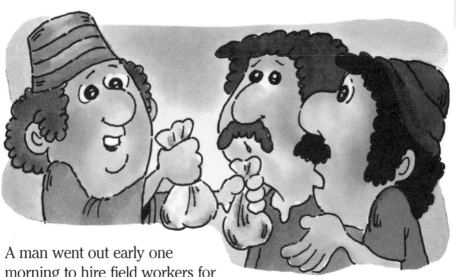

A man went out early one morning to hire field workers for the day. He agreed to pay them $20 for a whole day of work.

A few hours later he was in town again and hired some more men. Three more times throughout the day he hired more field workers. When the day was over all the men came to be payed. Those who worked only a few hours were paid the same as those who worked all day. The men who worked all day did not think that was fair. But the employer said, "Don't I have the right to do what I want with my money?"

Jesus taught that this is like God's forgiveness. No one deserves it. He gives it to us because he loves us, not because we have earned it. He gives it to anyone at any time who comes to him.

Why did the men who worked all day think the payment was not fair?

Why does God forgive us?

Dear God,
I am glad that I do not have to earn your grace. Thank you for giving it freely. Amen.

It is God's kindness that saved you. EPHESIANS 2:5

Jamie Forgives

CRASH!!! Mom's favorite lamp tumbled off the table and landed on the floor in several pieces. Mom hurried into the room. "What happened, Jamie?" she asked.

"I was parking my little cars under the table and I guess I bumped it. I'm really sorry. I know that was your favorite lamp," said Jamie, his eyes full of tears.

"Well, I can see it was an accident. I forgive you. Just let me pick up the glass before you continue playing," Mom said and she gave him a hug.

Later that day Mom asked Jamie if he wanted his friend Michael to come over. "No, he broke one of my cars. He's not my friend anymore," Jamie answered.

"Remember how I forgave you for the broken lamp? It feels good to be forgiven. Michael said he was sorry about the car. How about if you forgive him?"

What do you think Jamie did?

How do you feel when someone forgives you?

Dear God,
Help me be more forgiving. I want to be more like you. Help me remember to treat others the way I would like to be treated. Amen.

Be humble and gentle in every way. Be patient with each other and lovingly accept each other.
EPHESIANS 4:2

Sunday

A Wedding Banquet

MATTHEW 22:2-14

Jesus said the kingdom of heaven is like a king who gave a wedding banquet for his son. He sent a servant to bring the invited guests. But none of them would come. They all had more important things to do. In fact, some of them grabbed the messenger and killed him.

So the king said, "Since none of those we invited will come, just go out on the street and invite anyone you can find." Soon the wedding hall was full. The king was happy until he noticed a man who was not wearing wedding clothes. He asked the man why he was not properly dressed, the man had no answer. So the king said, "Tie up his hands and feet and throw him outside. Many are invited but few are chosen."

This story shows the judgment which all who reject God are going to face. It is important to love God deep in your heart, not just on the surface.

Who is the king in the story supposed to be?
Would you like to go to the banquet?

Dear God,
Thank you that people who love you are invited to heaven. Thank you for loving me. I love you. Amen.

The LORD is great. He should be highly praised. PSALM 48:1

Monday

Waiting for the Bridegroom

MATTHEW 25:1-13

The Kingdom of heaven is like ten brides who were waiting for their bridegroom to come. Five of the brides were wise and went out with lamps full of oil to wait for the bridegroom to come. Five brides were foolish and took lamps but no oil for them. It was a long time until the bridegroom came and the brides all fell asleep. Around midnight it was announced that the bridegroom was coming. The brides all jumped up and lit their lamps. The foolish brides begged the others to share their oil. But they said no. So the foolish brides ran to get some oil. While they were gone the bridegroom came. The five wise brides went into the banquet with him and the door was closed. When the foolish brides returned they shouted, "Let us in!" But the bridegroom said, "I don't know you."

Just like the brides we should always be watching for Jesus to return. We should always be ready.

Are you ready for Jesus to return?
How can you get ready?

Dear God,
Thank you for the reminder to always be ready for Jesus to come back. Thank you that I can watch for his return. Amen.

So stay awake, because you don't know the day or the hour.

MATTHEW 25:13

The Loan

MATT. 25:14-30; LUKE 19:12-27

Jesus taught about a man who loaned $5,000 to one servant, $2,000 to another, and $1,000 to another. Then he left on a trip.

The first two servants invested the money. So by the time the man returned the first servant had $10,000 and the second had $4,000. But the third servant was afraid of losing the money, so he buried his $1,000. He had only that to return to the man. The man was angry with him for not even putting it in the bank to get interest. He took the $1,000 away and gave it to the man with $10,000.

You should use whatever gifts and abilities God has given you to serve him. If you do not use them for him, they may be taken away.

What gifts and abilities do you have?

How can you use them to serve God?

Dear God,
Thank you for giving me the abilities I have. Help me to see ways I can do things for you. Amen.

Serve eagerly as if you were serving your heavenly master and not merely serving human masters. EPHESIANS 6:7

223

The Two Sons

MATT. 21:28-32

Jesus told a story about obeying. There was once a man who had two sons. He went to the first son and asked him to go work in the vineyards for him. The son said, "No!" But later he changed his mind and went anyway.

Then the man asked the second son to go work in the vineyards. This son said, "OK," but he did not go. Which son really obeyed his father?

We are disobeying God when we say we will do what he wants, but we do not do it.

When have you disobeyed your parents?
How do you feel when you do not obey?

Dear God,
Help me to mean what I say.
Help me to obey and live for you
as I have said I will. Amen.

Why do you call me Lord but don't do what I tell you? LUKE 6:46

Rich Fool

LUKE 12:16-21

Some people spend all their energy trying to earn more and more money. They think that is what life is all about.

Jesus told about a farmer who grew many crops. He didn't know what to do with them, so he tore down his barns and built bigger barns. Then he said, "Now I can just have fun. I have plenty of food to last many years. I do not have to work anymore."

This man was not thinking about God at all. He might die that very night and not know God.

Is money more important than knowing God?

How can you make God important in your life?

Dear God,
I want to learn more of your word. Help me to study it more.
Amen.

Your heart will be where your treasure is.   MATTHEW 6:21

225

The Lost Coin

LUKE 15:8-10

Suppose a woman had ten silver coins and she lost one. Do you think she would look for the lost coin? Yes, she would turn on all the lights and sweep her floor. She would look everywhere for it. Then when she found it, she would call all her friends so they could share in her happiness.

That's the kind of happiness there is in heaven when a sinner turns to God. The angels are filled with joy over that one person joining God's family.

What have you lost before that was special?

How does it feel to know the angels are happy when someone comes to God?

Dear God,
I feel very special to you. I'm glad I am part of your family. Amen.

God's angels are happy about one person who changes the way he thinks and acts.   LUKE 15:10

Jamie Learns a Lesson

Jamie and Dad were at the beach building a sand castle. Dad put the finishing touches on as Jamie dug a moat.

When they were finished they went to eat lunch. After lunch, Dad said, "The tide is going to be coming in, Jamie. You should pick up your sand toys, or they will drift out into the water."

"OK," said Jamie. But he rested on the sand for awhile after that. When he did finally go to pick up his toys, they were gone. Jamie ran to get Dad, "My toys are gone!" he cried.

"The waves of water came in and carried them away," answered Dad.

"Oh," said Jamie.

"They are gone because you did not obey. Just saying 'OK', but not actually doing what I told you to do, wasn't good enough."

Do you obey with words or actions?

When was a time that you wished you had obeyed?

Dear God,
Help me obey right away. Thank you for your help. Amen.

Love the Lord your God with all your heart, with all your soul, and with all your strength.

DEUTERONOMY 6:5

More Stories Jesus Told

The Good Samaritan

LUKE 10:30-37

Once a lawyer asked Jesus how to get eternal life. Jesus told him to love his neighbor as much as he loved himself. There were some people whom the man did not want to love, so he asked, "Which neighbor?"

Jesus explained with this story: "A Jewish man was going to Jericho when he was attacked by robbers. They took his money and his clothes and left him on the road to die. A priest came along, but he did not help the man. He crossed the road. A church helper came along, but he did not help the man either. Then a man from Samaria came by. Samaritans and Jews did not get along. But, he helped the man anyway. He put bandages on the man's wounds. Then he took him to a hotel and cared for him. Which man was a good neighbor?"

Which man do you think was a good neighbor?

Do you know people who are different? How do you feel about them?

Dear God,
Help me to love all people,
whether we are alike or different.
Amen.

Love your neighbor as you love yourself.   LEVITICUS 19:18

The Runaway Son

LUKE 15:11-32

Some church leaders said mean things about Jesus because he spent time with dishonest people. They didn't know how to forgive. Jesus taught them about forgiveness with this story: A man had two sons. The younger son wanted to leave home. So he asked his father for his share of the family money. Then he went to another country where he wasted the money. When the money was gone, the son was alone with no job and no food. He took a job feeding pigs. But soon he wondered if he could go home and beg for his dad's forgiveness. Then maybe his dad would hire him as a fieldhand.

The boy started for home. As soon as the dad saw his son, he ran out and hugged him. The father arranged a big party to welcome his son home. The father would have lost his son if he had not been able to forgive him.

When have you had to ask for forgiveness?
What did the person you asked for forgiveness say?

Dear God,
Forgive me for the times I am selfish. Forgive me for judging other people. Help me live more like you. Amen.

Forgive as the Lord forgave you.
COLOSSIANS 3:13

A Friend in Need

LUKE 11:5-8

Jesus' disciples once asked him how to pray. One thing Jesus taught about prayer was to pray continually. This is the story he told: Suppose you went to a friend's house at midnight to borrow some bread. You tell your friend that you have company but you do not have any food for them. Your friend says, "I'm already in bed. Wait until morning." But you do not want to wait, so you keep knocking on his door and calling to him. He will finally get up and give you the bread.

It is the same way with prayer. When something is important, keep asking God for it.

What things are you praying for now?
When you pray for something, do you believe God will answer?

Dear God,
Thank you for examples of how to pray. Help me learn to pray better. Amen.

Ask, and you will receive. Search, and you will find. Knock, and the door will be opened for you. LUKE 11:9

The Widow Who Did Not Give Up

LUKE 18:2-8

Jesus told his disciples a story showing that when they pray, they should not give up if they do not get an answer right away.

A woman whose husband had died kept going to see a judge about a man who had been unfair to her. This judge did not believe in God and he did not care about anyone. But the woman kept coming to him. He kept refusing to do anything. Finally he said to himself, *I'm going to give this woman justice because she keeps coming to me.*

If a man like that will give justice, don't you think God will certainly give even more to his people who ask?

What have you prayed about for a long time?
Do you ever want to give up?

Dear God,
Waiting for your answer is hard sometimes. Help me to keep praying and believing that you will answer. Amen.

Never stop praying.
1 THESSALONIANS 5:17

The Pharisee and the Tax Collector

LUKE 18:9-14

Some people think they are better than other people. Jesus had a story for them. He said, "Two men went to the temple to pray. One was a Pharisee, (a church leader) the other was a tax collector. The Pharisee stood up tall and prayed aloud, 'O God, thank you that I am not like other people who rob and steal — like that tax collector over there. I go without food two times a week and I give money to the church. I am so good!'

"Then the tax collector prayed quietly, he did not even lift his head. He prayed, 'O God, forgive me. I am a sinner.' "

Jesus said, "The tax collector went home forgiven, the Pharisee did not."

Which man showed he was sorry for his sins?
Do you ever feel like you are better than others?

Dear God,
Sometimes I do feel a little better than others. But I am sorry for my sins. Please forgive me. Amen.

Everyone who honors himself will be humbled, but the person who humbles himself will be honored.   LUKE 18:14

Good Fish vs. Bad Fish

MATTHEW 13:47-50

Jesus told another story that showed what the kingdom of heaven is like. It would be like a fisherman who dropped his net into the water. When he pulled the net up it was full of all kinds of fish. So the fisherman sat down and emptied the net. The fish that were good to eat he put in a box. But, the fish that were not good to eat he threw back into the water.

That is how it will be at the judgment. The angels will look at all people and separate them. Those who know God will go to heaven. But those who do not know him, will not.

Will you go to heaven just because your parents do?
Will you go to heaven because you are a nice person?

Dear God,
The only way to get to heaven is to believe in Jesus Christ and accept him as my savior. Thank you that there is a way. Amen.

The Son of Man must be lifted up. Then everyone who believes in him will have eternal life.

JOHN 3:14-15

Who Is My Neighbor?

"Jamie, want to come with me? I am going to take a cake over to our new neighbor," Mom called upstairs.

Jamie came running down. "Can I have some cake?" he asked.

"No," Mom laughed. "It's to welcome our new neighbors."

"Why? They are from another country and they barely even speak English. They won't be very good friends if we can't talk to them," Jamie said.

"Jamie, we shouldn't be friends only with people who are like us. Now we have a good chance to meet some interesting people."

Did Jamie understand who his neighbors are?
Do you have any friends from another country? Who?

Dear God,
Help me be friends with people who are different. Help me be a good neighbor. Amen.

We should all be concerned about our neighbor and the good things that will build his faith.

ROMANS 15:2

Followers of Jesus

Sunday

Simon and Andrew

MATT. 4:18-22; MARK 1:16-20; JOHN 1:35-42

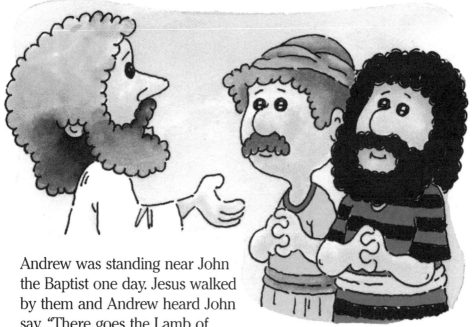

Andrew was standing near John the Baptist one day. Jesus walked by them and Andrew heard John say, "There goes the Lamb of God!" Andrew and another man ran after Jesus and talked with him for quite a while. After that Andrew ran to find his brother Simon. He said, "Come and see. We have found the Messiah!"

Later Jesus was walking near the Sea of Galilee. He saw Simon and Andrew fishing. That was how they earned their livings. Jesus said, "Follow me and I will make you fishers of men." Simon and Andrew dropped their nets and followed Jesus.

Who did Andrew tell about Jesus?

What does "fishers of men" mean?

Dear God,
Being a fisher of men means telling others about you. Give me chances to tell my friends about your love. Amen.

Come, follow me! I will teach you how to catch people instead of fish!   MARK 1:17

235

Levi

MATT. 9:9-13; MARK 2:14-17; LUKE 5:27-32

Jesus was teaching a large crowd of people. He saw Levi, a tax collector, sitting at a table collecting money. Jesus went over to Levi and said, "Follow me." Levi got right up and followed Jesus.

Then Jesus went to Levi's house for dinner. Levi invited many of his tax collector friends to meet Jesus. Some church leaders saw Jesus eating with these dishonest people. They said he should not be with them. But Jesus came for all people. He knows that everyone needs him.

What was the first thing Levi did after meeting Jesus?

Who have you invited to Sunday School or church?

Dear God,
Help me be brave and excited about telling other people about you. Amen.

I've come to call sinners, not people without any flaws.

MARK 2:17

John the Baptist

MATTHEW 3:1-16; MARK 1:2-13; LUKE 3:2-10

John the Baptist lived in the desert and dressed in clothes made of camel's hair. He traveled around preaching that people should stop sinning and be baptized. He was getting the people ready to hear what Jesus had to say.

One day John the Baptist was baptizing people in a river. Jesus came and asked John to baptize him. John knew that Jesus is the Son of God. So he said, "No, you should baptize me." But Jesus kept asking, so John baptized him. As soon as Jesus came out of the water, a voice from heaven said, "This is my Son and I love him."

John spent all his time telling others about Jesus. How much time do you spend telling others?
Have you been baptized?

Dear God,
John devoted his whole life to telling others about you. Help me to tell just one today. Amen.

Prepare the way for the Lord! Make his paths straight!

MATTHEW 3:3

237

Peter

MATTHEW 14:22-33

Peter was a fisherman who followed Jesus. He was very eager to tell others about Jesus because he loved Jesus very much.

One night when the disciples were in a boat crossing a lake, Jesus walked on top of the water to join them. The disciples were afraid when they saw the man coming, but Jesus told them it was him. Peter said, "Lord, if it is you, let me come to you on the water."

Jesus said, "Come on." So Peter walked on top of the water.

But when he saw the wind and waves around him, he got scared and started to sink. "Save me!" he cried.

Jesus grabbed his hand and pulled him up. "Why didn't you have faith?" Jesus asked. Then they got in the boat and all the disciples worshiped Jesus.

Do you think Peter was brave?

How can you tell that Peter loved Jesus?

Dear God,
Peter is a good example of a person who loves you. Help me be brave enough to take a stand for you like Peter. Amen.

May goodwill and peace prevail in your lives through your knowledge about Jesus, our God and Lord!   2 PETER 1:2

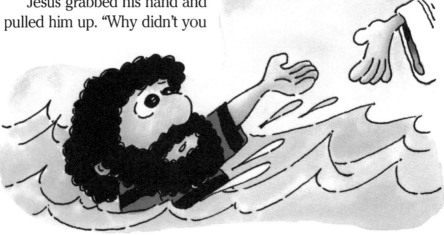

The Woman with Perfume

MATTHEW 26:6-13

When Jesus was at Simon's house a woman came in. She carried a fancy jar of expensive perfume. While Jesus was sitting at the table, the woman poured the perfume on his head. The disciples got angry. "Why is she wasting such expensive perfume?" they asked. "We could have sold the perfume and given the money to the poor."

Jesus knew they did not understand the future as well as the woman did. She knew that the poor would always be around. But Jesus was only going to be with them a short time. Pouring the perfume on him was her way of getting him ready to die.

Why were the disciples upset?

What did the woman know that the disciples didn't?

Dear God,
The woman really knew how to honor you. Help me to honor you in my life. Amen.

You will always have the poor with you, but you will not always have me with you.   JOHN 12:8

Zacchaeus
LUKE 19:1-10

Zacchaeus was a tax collector in Jericho. He didn't have many friends. No one liked tax collectors because they cheated people. Zacchaeus heard that Jesus was coming to town. He had heard of the wonderful things Jesus did.

Zacchaeus thought, *I would like to see Jesus when he comes.* But Zacchaeus was a short man. It would be hard for him to see Jesus over the crowd. Then Zacchaeus had a great idea: he would climb a tree and be able to see Jesus over the crowd.

Jesus saw Zacchaeus in the tree and told him to come down. Jesus wanted to go to his house.

After they talked for awhile Zacchaeus said he would never cheat people again and he would pay back all the people from whom he had stolen.

Why couldn't Zacchaeus see Jesus?

Why did Zacchaeus want to pay people back?

Dear God,
Zacchaeus changed after he talked to Jesus. The more time I spend with you the more I will change to be like you. Amen.

The Son of Man has come to seek and to save people who are lost. LUKE 19:10

Jamie Follows Jesus

"Mom, can I invite Tommy to come to Vacation Bible School with me?" Jamie asked. "He doesn't go to church anywhere and I think he needs to hear about Jesus," he added.

"Jamie, you are being a follower of Jesus," Mom said. "Just like the people we read about who knew Jesus. Each of them met Jesus, then wanted to tell someone else about him, or do something for him."

How do you think Jamie felt about being a follower of Jesus?

Do you think Jesus is important in Jamie's life?

*Dear God,
I want to be a follower of yours too. I want to tell others that you love them. I want to bring my friends to Sunday school and church. Amen.*

You are Christ's body and each of you is an individual part of it.
1 CORINTHIANS 12:27

How Should We Live Together?

Relating to Each Other

EPHESIANS 4:25-32

The best way to live together is to treat others the way you want them to treat you. Do not lie to each other. Lying hurts your friends and makes them angry.

Try not to get mad at others, but when you do settle it quickly. Don't ignore your anger and go to bed while you are still mad.

Don't use bad language. Say things that will help others and encourage them.

Remember to be kind to each other. Forgive others when they make mistakes, because God has forgiven your mistakes.

How do you feel when someone is unkind to you?

How do you feel when you are kind to a friend?

Dear God,
Help me remember to treat others the way I would like to be treated. That will make life more pleasant. Amen.

Everyone must live in harmony.
1 PETER 3:8

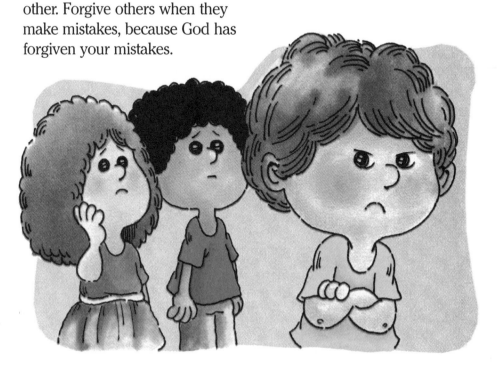

Copy God

Ephesians 5:1-5

Learn everything you can about God and copy everything you know. Try to be as much like him as you can. Don't keep bad thoughts in your mind and don't be greedy or selfish. God would not live that way and neither should you. Don't use bad language or say mean things about others. Instead use your voice to praise God and thank him for all he has given you.

Only people who are trying to live like God will be allowed into his kingdom, heaven. Those who enjoy keeping bad thoughts inside them and saying bad things about others will not be allowed into his kingdom.

How can you learn about God?

How can you use your voice to praise God?

Dear God,
Thank you for help in knowing how to live like you. Thank you for having someone write these things down. Amen.

Imitate God, since you are the children he loves.

Ephesians 5:1

243

Tuesday

Live in the Light

EPHESIANS 5:8-14

People who love Jesus are not the same as people who do not know him. Others can look at you and see good and fairness and truth because you live for Jesus. You will learn as you go along, what makes God happy. You will learn more about how to live for him.

Do not have anything to do with people who do not know God and who want to do bad things. Instead point out those bad things and help people want to choose Jesus instead.

Jesus is like a light that shines through his people. When we meet people who do not know him, that light shows them how they are living. That may make them want to come to Jesus

How are you different from other people?
What about you is different because you know Jesus?

Dear God,
I want my friends to know I am different because I love you. Help me to treat my friends and family the way you want me to. Amen.

Be very careful how you live. Don't live like foolish people but like people who are wise.

EPHESIANS 5:15

Use Good Sense

EPHESIANS 5:15-20

Everyday there are choices to make. You choose to be in a good mood or bad mood. You choose to be kind or unkind. You choose to use your time wisely or unwisely. Be sure you make good choices. Make the most of every opportunity. Do good as much as you can. Talk to God often so you know what he wants you to do.

Praise God with others who love him. Sing praise to him, aloud and in your heart. Thank God for everything.

When have you made a wise choice?

What would you like to thank God for?

Dear God,
Help me to make good choices.
Thank you for all the things you
have given me and done for me.
Amen.

Live in love.

EPHESIANS 5:2

245

Thursday

Children Obey Parents

EPHESIANS 6:1-3

Your parents love you very much. They want the best for you. Sometimes it is not easy for them to teach you how to act and how to treat others. But they want to teach you about God and how to live in a way that is pleasing to him.

It may not always be the fun thing, but the right thing for you to do is obey your parents. God says, "Honor your father and mother." When you respect them and obey them your home will be more peaceful and you will have a longer and happier life. Someday when you are a mom or dad, you will know how to teach your children.

Are you good at obeying your mom or dad?
What do you need to change to be more honoring to them?

Dear God,
Thank you for my parents. I know they do their best to teach me about you and how to be a good person. Help me to be more obedient. Amen.

Children, always obey your parents. This is pleasing to the Lord.   COLOSSIANS 3:20

The Armor of God

EPHESIANS 6:10-25

Remember you do not have to try to be good by yourself. God knows that Satan will be trying to stop you. You can get the strength to do right from God. He has provided a suit of armor that you can wear to protect yourself from Satan. Put on the vest of truth and the breastplate of righteousness. Carry the shield of faith. Wear the helmet of salvation and use the sword of the Spirit, which is God's Word.

And it is very important to pray all the time. God is happy to hear all kinds of prayers and requests. Pray for yourself and for other believers.

How can you put on God's suit of armor?

Who do you pray for besides yourself?

Dear God,
Thank you for the pieces of armor I can use for protection. Thank you that I can pray to you about anything. Amen.

Receive your power from the Lord and from his mighty strength. EPHESIANS 6:10

Jamie Is Angry

SLAM!!!!! STOMP!!!! STOMP!!! Jamie was home and he was not happy. He slammed doors and stomped around the house. He even tried to kick the cat out of his way. Although, when Mom asked about that, he said he just gave her a gentle push with his foot. Finally Mom went to talk to Jamie. "What's wrong?" she asked.

"I am so MAD at Tommy!" Jamie shouted. "He wouldn't let me play with his new mini-cars. I don't ever want to play with him again!"

"Did you tell him that you would be careful?" Mom asked.

"Yes. He just didn't want to share," Jamie answered.

"Why don't you go talk to him about it? Remember what God tells us. When we are angry at someone we should settle it quickly. I'm sure there is a happy way to settle this."

What do you think Jamie said to Tommy?

When have you been angry with someone?

Dear God,
It's no fun to be mad at my friends. Help me be brave enough to talk to them about things I am upset about. Amen.

Don't go to bed angry.

EPHESIANS 4:26

The Last Days of Jesus

Sunday

Predicting His Death

MATTHEW 16:21-29; MARK 8:31—9:1; LUKE 9:22-27

Jesus knew what was going to happen to him on earth before he even came here. When he was 30 years old he began teaching about God. He healed sick people and raised people from the dead. But he never forgot what was ahead for him.

Three different times when Jesus was speaking, He told his followers that many terrible things were going to happen to him. He told them that he was going to suffer and die. He also told them that on the third day after he died, he would be raised from the dead.

What terrible things happened to Jesus?

Why did Jesus come, knowing what was going to happen?

Dear God,
Thank you that Jesus was willing to come to earth even though he knew the terrible things that would happen to him here. I couldn't be talking to you now if he didn't come. Amen.

The Son of Man would have to suffer a lot. . . . He would be killed, but on the third day he would come back to life.

LUKE 9:22

Triumphal Entry

MATT. 21:1-11; MARK 11:1-10; LUKE 19:28-38; JOHN 12:12-15

like a king, but in just a short time some of these same people would be shouting "Crucify him!"

It was time to go to Jerusalem. Terrible things would happen there. Jesus would be killed. He sent two of his followers ahead to get a young donkey for him to ride as he went into the city.

As Jesus rode into the city on the donkey, crowds gathered along the road shouting, "Hosanna to the Son of David!" Some laid their coats or palm branches on the ground for him to ride over. They treated him

What did people lay on the road that Jesus rode down?

Why did the people shout as he rode into Jerusalem?

Dear God,
It must have made Jesus sad to hear people cheer and know that later they would want him to die. Jesus was very brave. Amen.

Hosanna! Blessed is the one who comes in the name of the Lord!

JOHN 12:13

The Betrayal

MATTHEW 26:14-16; MARK 14:10-11; LUKE 22:3-6

Some of the church leaders were upset because Jesus did not keep all their rules. Also they did not like the fact that he was so popular. The church leaders looked for ways to get Jesus in trouble, but they had to be careful because of the crowds that loved him.

One of Jesus' own disciples was the answer to their problems. Judas Iscariot made a deal with the church leaders. He agreed to turn Jesus over to them in the middle of the night. They paid Judas thirty pieces of silver to tell them where Jesus was. Judas told them to watch which man he greeted with a kiss on the cheek. That man would be Jesus. Then they could arrest him.

Why didn't the church leaders like Jesus?

How much money did Judas get to betray him?

Dear God,
It must have hurt even more that a friend turned Jesus in. I feel so sad that all of this happened to him. But I am so thankful that he was willing to go through it. Amen.

They offered him 30 silver coins. From then on, he looked for a chance to betray Jesus.

MATTHEW 26:15-16

The Last Supper

MATTHEW 26:17-30; MARK 14:12-26; LUKE 22:7-22

Jesus and his disciples celebrated the Passover together in a small upstairs room. The disciples fixed dinner. While they were eating, Jesus told them that one of them was going to betray him. Each of them wondered who would do such a terrible thing.

Jesus took the loaf of bread, broke it in pieces and thanked God for it. As he gave it to his friends, he said, "Eat this, it is my body." Then he took the wine and thanked God for it. He passed it around and said, "Drink this, it is my blood which will be poured out for many." Jesus was talking about his death which would be for all people.

Which disciple was going to betray Jesus?

If you were a disciple, how would you have felt about what Jesus said?

Dear God,
The disciples must have been confused when Jesus said these things. They didn't know how close his death was. Thank you for helping me understand how Jesus' death makes it possible for me to know you. Amen.

This is my blood, the blood of the promise. It is poured out for humanity.　　　MARK 14:24

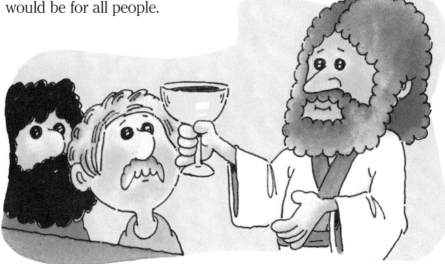

Crucify Him!

MATTHEW 27:11-56; MARK 15:2-41; LUKE 23:2-49

Jesus was arrested after Judas kissed him on the cheek. He was taken to Pilate, the governor. Pilate told the people that he could free one prisoner for the Passover celebration. He thought the people would want Jesus freed. But the crowd shouted, "Crucify him!" So he gave Jesus to the soldiers to be beaten and nailed to a cross.

Even while Jesus was on the cross he was thinking about others. He asked God to forgive the people who were hurting him.

Jesus died on the cross for us. If we believe in him we can live in heaven with him someday.

How do you feel about the crowd wanting Jesus to die?

Do you know that you are going to heaven someday?

Dear God,
I know it was part of your plan to have this all happen to Jesus. Thank you for making a plan that makes it possible for me to come to heaven. Amen.

In this way God loved the world; He gave his only son so that everyone who believes in him will not die but will have eternal life.   JOHN 3:16

Friday

Jesus Is Buried

MATTHEW 27:57-61; MARK 15:42-47; LUKE 23:50-56; JOHN 19:38-42

A man named Joseph asked if he could take Jesus' body. Joseph believed Jesus was the Son of God, but did not want to let many people know that. He was a rich man and a member of the governing council. He was afraid of what the Jews would do to him if they knew he believed.

Pilate gave the body to Joseph. He took it and wrapped it in a clean linen cloth. Then he buried Jesus in a new tomb. A huge stone was rolled in front of the entrance. A seal was put on the stone so they could tell if anyone tried to move it. Guards stood in front of the stone. The Jews wanted to be sure that no one tried to steal Jesus' body.

Why was Joseph afraid to say he believed in Jesus? What was done to be sure no one stole the body?

Dear God,
That must have been a very sad day for all of Jesus' followers. Thank you that Joseph took Jesus and buried him. Amen.

After he took [the body] down from the cross, he wrapped it in linen. Then he laid the body in a tomb cut in rock, a tomb in which no one had ever been buried. LUKE 23:53

Jamie Asks, "Why?"

"Those people were mean. Why did they do those things to Jesus? He didn't do anything to them. I hope none of them got to go to heaven!" Jamie said.

"It sure seems like they were mean, doesn't it? But really, everything that happened to Jesus was part of God's wonderful plan," Dad explained. "A long time ago Adam and Eve sinned and that meant that all people after them were sinners too. God does not allow sin in heaven, so he made a plan. The plan was that his Son would come to earth and die for our sins. Then if we believe Jesus is God's Son, that he died for us, and that he rose from the dead, we can go to heaven someday."

"I am really glad for that plan," Jamie said snuggling on Dad's lap.

Why did God have to make this plan?
Is there someone you would like to tell about God's plan?

Dear God,
Thank you for your wonderful plan. I am glad to know that I can come to heaven and live with you someday. I want to tell everyone! Amen.

God didn't send his son into the world to judge the world. Instead, he sent his son to save the world.
JOHN 3:17

255

He Is Alive!

The Empty Tomb

MATT. 28:1-8; MARK 16:1-8; LUKE 24:1-10; JOHN 20:1-9

After Jesus was buried two of his women followers went to the tomb to put spices and perfumes on his body. That was their custom. But they didn't know how they were going to move the big stone that was in front of the door.

When they got to the tomb, they were surprised! The stone was already moved! Even more amazing, Jesus' body was gone! Two angels were sitting in the tomb. They told the women, "Jesus is not here. He is risen!" Jesus was alive!

Was Jesus rising from the dead part of God's plan too?

How do you think the women felt?

*Dear God,
Hurrah! The plan wouldn't have been any good without this happy ending! Thank you that Jesus is alive! Amen.*

He's not here. He has been brought back to life as he said.
MATTHEW 28:6

Mary Sees Jesus

JOHN 20:10-18

Everybody left the empty tomb and went back to town. Everybody except Mary. She stood there, crying. She wanted to know where Jesus' body was. Then a man came and asked her why she was crying. Mary thought he was the gardener so she said, "Did you take him? Tell me where he is and I will get him." The man said, "Mary." Suddenly Mary knew the man was Jesus! He said, "Don't touch me. I haven't returned to my Father yet. Go find my disciples and tell them I am going back to my Father." Mary ran to tell the disciples that she had seen Jesus and what he had told her.

Why was Mary crying? Where was Jesus going?

Dear God,
Thank you that Jesus rose from the dead. Thank you that he is alive today! Amen.

I will still be with you for a little while. Then I'll go to the one who sent me.

JOHN 7:33

257

The Road to Emmaus

LUKE 24:13-35

Two of Jesus' followers were on their way to Emmaus. They walked along slowly, talking about everything that had happened. As they walked Jesus came up and walked with them. But they did not know it was Jesus. "What are you talking about?" he asked. They explained all that had happened .

When they got to Emmaus, they asked him to come in and they served dinner. The man gave thanks for the food and, suddenly, they knew he was Jesus. But as soon as they knew, he disappeared! Then they told each other how their hearts had been moved while he talked with them on the road. They hurried to tell the other disciples!

Why didn't the disciples know Jesus?

How did they feel when they knew it was Jesus?

Dear God,
Those men must have been so excited. Now they could believe Jesus was alive because they saw him in person. Amen.

The Lord has really come back to life.

LUKE 24:34

Doubting Thomas

JOHN 20:24-29

One time all the disciples except Thomas were together and Jesus came to see them. Since he did not see Jesus himself, Thomas would not believe Jesus was alive. He wanted to see Jesus. He wanted to touch Jesus' wounds.

A week later the disciples were all together again and this time Thomas was with them. Jesus came to them. He let Thomas touch his hands and side where the wounds were. Then Thomas believed Jesus was alive again.

Jesus was glad Thomas believed. He was even happier because of the people who have not seen him and still believe.

Why wouldn't Thomas believe Jesus was alive?

Who was Jesus talking about who believed without seeing?

Dear God,
Thank you that I believe even though I haven't actually seen you. Thank you for your patience with Thomas. Amen.

Blessed are those who have not seen me and yet have become believers.

JOHN 20:29

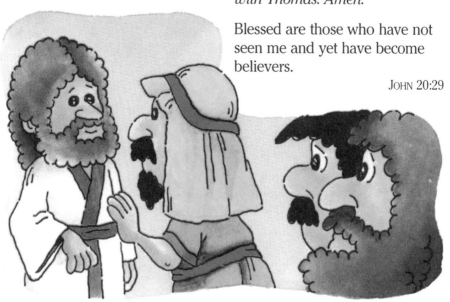

Breakfast with Friends

JOHN 21:4-14

Peter and his friends had been fishing all night. But they didn't catch anything. Early in the morning, they came back to shore. A man was standing there that Peter did not know. He asked, "Do you have any fish?"

"No, we didn't catch any," Peter answered.

"Well, if you throw your nets out on the other side, you will catch some," he said.

Peter was too tired to argue. They threw out their nets and caught over a hundred fish. "Bring some fish to me," the man said. Suddenly, the disciples knew the man was Jesus. He gave them bread and fish and they all had breakfast together. This was the third time Jesus appeared to his disciples since he arose from the dead.

Who was the man standing on shore?

How many times did the disciples see Jesus after he arose?

Dear God,
It must have made the disciples feel so much better when they saw Jesus. I'm glad they got to see him. Amen.

They knew it was the Lord.

JOHN 21:12

The Ascension

LUKE 24:50-53; ACTS 1:1-11

"What are you looking at?" they asked. "Jesus has just gone back to heaven. He will come back some day in a cloud, just as he left."

One last time Jesus was eating with his disciples after the resurrection. He told them that the Holy Spirit would soon come and give them God's power. Jesus wanted them to tell people everywhere about him. Not just people in the town where they lived. He wanted them to go all over the world to tell about him.

After Jesus gave the disciples their final instructions, he was taken up to heaven. Right in front of their eyes, he went up into a cloud.

They were all staring up at the sky when two angels came.

Where did Jesus want the disciples to preach about him?

How is Jesus going to come back some day?

Dear God,
I guess you want me to tell people everywhere about your love too. Help me to stay busy doing that until Jesus comes back. Amen.

You will be my witnesses to testify about me in Jerusalem, throughout Judea and Samaria, and to the ends of the earth.

ACTS 1:8

261

Happy Easter!

"Yeaaa!!!! It's Easter Sunday. This is my favorite holiday," Jamie announced. "I like the Easter baskets, and the new clothes, and the big dinner, and that summer is coming. Why do we celebrate Easter anyway?" Jamie asked.

"Remember the stories we've read about Jesus' death and how he came back to life?" Mom asked.

"Yes," answered Jamie.

"We celebrate Easter as the day Jesus rose from the dead. It's a very important part of our faith. Easter morning showed that Jesus had won over death."

What is your favorite part of Easter?

What is the most important part of Easter?

Dear God,
Thank you for Easter Sunday. It was one of the last steps in your great plan. I'm glad I can go to heaven someday because of Easter. Amen.

Christ died to take away our sins as the Scriptures predicted. He was placed in a tomb. He was brought back to life on the third day as the Scriptures predicted.
1 CORINTHIANS 15:3-4

Serving the Lord

Sunday

Dorcas

Acts 9:36-42

Dorcas was a very kind lady. She did good things for people. She helped poor people. One way Dorcas helped others was by making robes and clothing for them. Many people loved Dorcas. They saw God's love in the way she lived.

One day Dorcas got sick and died. Her friends were very sad. They sent for Peter. He came and saw everyone crying. They showed him the clothing Dorcas had made for them.

Peter sent them away and he knelt and prayed. Then he said, "Dorcas, get up!" She did! God helped Peter bring her back to life. Everyone was so happy!

How did Dorcas show God's love to others?

How can you show God's love to others?

Dear God,
I am glad to read about Dorcas and how she served God by being kind. Please help me be kind to others too. Amen.

If this is the way God loved us, we must also love each other.

1 John 4:11

Monday

Serving God by Serving Others

MATTHEW 25:31–40

Is serving God something that only grown-ups can do? Is the only way to serve God by teaching Sunday School or being a minister or a missionary?

Those are some ways to serve God. But Jesus said that another way of serving him is by serving others. Serving others can be giving food to hungry people, a drink to thirsty people, being kind to strangers, giving clothes to people who have none, taking care of the sick, and visiting people in prison. Jesus said that doing these things for other people is the same as doing them for him.

Which of these things have you helped to do?

How can you serve others?

Dear God,
There are people everywhere who need help. Show me ways that I can serve you by serving others. Amen.

The King will answer them, "I can guarantee this truth: Whatever you did for one of my brothers or sisters, no matter how unimportant they seemed, you did it for me.

MATTHEW 25:40

The Woman Who Gave Everything

MARK 12:41-44

When a rich person gives a lot of money to God's work, many people praise him. They say, "He is so wonderful. He gave so much money to God's work." The rich person did give a lot of money, but he had a lot money left to live on.

Jesus was in the temple when a poor woman came in. She put two coins in the offering. They were not even worth a penny. But Jesus said that she gave more than any rich person. That was because she gave all she had to live on.

Why did Jesus say the poor woman gave more than the rich man?

How much do you give to God's work?

Dear God,
I want to give to your work. Help me remember to take some of my money to put in the Sunday School offering. Amen.

All of them have given what they could spare. But she, in her poverty, has given everything she had to live on.

MARK 12:44

265

Philip Obeys

ACTS 8:26-39

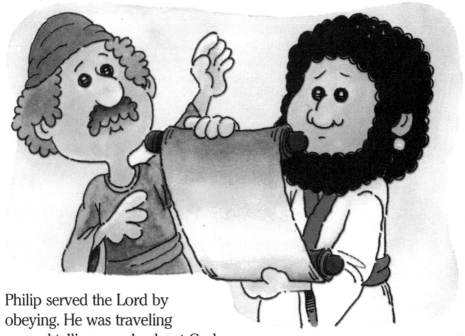

Philip served the Lord by obeying. He was traveling around telling people about God, when an angel told him to go down a certain road. Philip obeyed, and on that road he met a man who was reading the Bible. But the man did not understand what he was reading. So Philip sat down with him and explained that the Bible was talking about how Jesus died for our sins so that we can know God. The man believed and asked Jesus to come into his heart. They stopped and Philip baptized him right there beside the road.

Did Philip ask why he should obey the angel?

How do you serve God by obeying?

Dear God,
I can serve you by obeying my parents without questioning. Help me to be a good servant. Amen.

Philip . . . told the official the Good News about Jesus.

ACTS 8:35

Stephen

Acts 6

Stephen loved God very much. He told many people about God. But some people who did not love God got very mad at Stephen. They arrested him and said that he did bad things. They tried to get other people mad at him too.

Finally so many people were angry at Stephen that they decided to kill him. Stephen wasn't afraid, though. Even while they were killing him, his face looked like an angel's face. As he died, he asked God to forgive the people who were hurting him. Stephen served God right until the minute he died.

Why did people get mad at Stephen?

Who can you tell about God's love?

Dear God,
Stephen was very brave. He was not even afraid to die for you. Help me to be that brave and to show others how much I love you. Amen.

So Stephen said, "Look, I see heaven opened and the Son of Man exercising the power that God has given him!"   Acts 7:56

A Second Chance

ACTS 15:36-41; COLOSSIANS 4:10-11; 2 TIMOTHY 4:11

Paul and Barnabas went on many trips to tell people in other places about Jesus. A young man named John Mark traveled with them one time. But, John Mark left them and went home in the middle of the trip.

Paul did not like that, so when he began planning another trip, he did not want John Mark to come along. He felt so strongly about this that he and Barnabas split up. Barnabas took John Mark with him and Paul took Silas on a different trip.

But a while later, Paul gave John Mark a second chance to travel with him. John Mark showed Paul that he was a good servant of God. He became a good friend of Paul and an important part of his ministry.

When has God given you a second chance after a mistake?

Are you willing to give others a second chance?

Dear God,
Thank you for your forgiveness
that gives me a second chance.
Help me to forgive others. Amen.

Whenever you pray, forgive anything you have against anyone. Then your Father in heaven will forgive your failures.
MARK 11:25

Jamie Serves God

TOYS FOR TOTS

"Mom I don't want to read any more stories about serving God," Jamie blurted out. "Those stories are all about things that grown-ups do, I'm just a kid and I can't serve God like a grown-up!"

"You're right, Jamie," Mom said. "Let's think about some way that you can serve God. Got any ideas?"

"Well, I did like the story about helping other people. I could help you when you take food to someone who is sick. I could clean out my toy box and take some toys to children who do not have any. There are many toys I do not play with anymore."

What do you think of Jamie's idea?
How can you serve God?

Dear God,
Everyone who loves you can do something for you. Help me see ways I can serve you. Amen.

Help carry each other's burdens. In this way you will follow Christ's teachings.

GALATIANS 6:2

269

The First Church

A Special Gift

ACTS 2:1-12

When Jesus was taken up to heaven, he promised to send a special gift to his followers. One time they were all together when they heard a loud sound like the wind blowing very hard. Suddenly they saw little flames of fire come and settle above each person's head.

This was Jesus' gift to them: the Holy Spirit. The Holy Spirit helped them to be strong for God. He helped them tell others about God's love. He was with each of them forever!

How do you think the people felt when the Holy Spirit came to them?

Do believers today have the Holy Spirit?

Dear God,
Thank you for the Holy Spirit. He makes me strong and brave for you. Thank you for his protection. Amen.

Each of you must be baptized in the name of Jesus Christ so that your sins will be forgiven. Then you will receive the Holy Spirit as a gift. ACTS 2:38

Doing God's Work

ACTS 3:1-10

One day when Peter and John were going to the temple to pray, they saw a man who could not walk. He was being carried to the doorway of the temple. When the man saw Peter and John he asked them for money. That was the only way he could get money for food.

Peter said, "I don't have any money to give you, but I have something much better. In the name of Jesus Christ of Nazareth, get up and walk." Then Peter took the man's hand and helped him stand up! For the first time in his life, the man could stand and walk! The man went into the temple, praising God.

How did Peter serve God?

Why did the man praise God?

Dear God,
It is exciting to see how Peter and John served you by helping the man. They didn't just give him money, they gave him what he really needed. Help me to see ways I can tell people about you. Amen.

Sing his praise. PSALM 149:1

Tuesday

Overcoming Trouble

Acts 5:17-42

Every day Jesus' followers, taught people about him. Every day God helped them heal sick people. Leaders of the old established church did not believe in Jesus. They were jealous of his followers. The church leaders got so angry that they had some of Jesus' followers arrested. But God sent an angel to get them out of jail.

The church leaders found them, and now they were angrier than ever. They wanted to kill Jesus' followers, but one man talked them out of it. So instead, they beat them. Then they said, "Stop talking about Jesus. Stop healing people in his name!"

When they let Jesus' followers go, they went right on telling everyone about him.

Have you ever been in trouble for talking about Jesus?
What would you do if someone told you not to talk about him?

Dear God,
Your followers were very brave, they didn't stop talking about Jesus. Make me brave enough to talk about you anywhere, anytime. Amen.

People from all nations (beginning with the city of Jerusalem) must be told that they need to change the way they think and act so that their sins will be forgiven.   Luke 24:47

Sharing with One Another

ACTS 2:42-47; 4:32-37

The members of the first church helped each other whenever there was a problem. They had to stick together because there were people who did not like them and even tried to stop their work.

If a member of the church needed money, other members would sell their belongings and give money to the person who needed it. They shared everything they had so there were no needy persons in the church. The apostles preached about Jesus and the church members were happy to be together.

How does your church help needy people?

Are you happy to be with your church family?

Dear God,
Show me how I can help someone who has a need. Help me to be sensitive to others.
Amen.

The whole group of believers lived in harmony.   ACTS 4:32

Miracles

ACTS 5:12-16

The apostles of Jesus met together every day in a certain place. Some of the other believers didn't join them, but they respected them very much. More and more people believed in Jesus because of their preaching and miracles. So more and more people came to hear them and see what was going on.

Sick people were brought out to the road on their mats and beds in hopes that Peter's shadow would fall on them as he went by. Then the sick person would be well. People came from towns all around bringing sick friends and relatives. Every one of them was healed!

Where did the apostles get the power to heal sick people?

Have you ever seen a miracle?

Dear God,
It sounds like the first church grew larger very quickly. It's important for your people to meet together and do your work. Then more people will want to know Jesus. Thank you that I can go to church. Amen.

More men and women than ever began to believe in the Lord.

ACTS 5:14

Sending out Missionaries

ACTS 13:1-5

The members of the first church stayed very busy telling others about Jesus and doing miracles. They wanted everyone to know about God's love. So when God told them to send Saul and Barnabas to another country to tell about him, they were happy to do so.

The church members prayed for Saul and Barnabas and then sent them to Cyprus. The two missionaries preached about God to people who had never heard about his love. They were the first missionaries to ever be sent out by a church.

Who are some missionaries from your church?

Have you heard missionaries speak at your church? From what country?

Dear God,
Thank you for caring about people in other countries. Help our missionaries be strong and not get tired. Give them many chances to tell others about you. Amen.

Go and make disciples of all nations: Baptizing them in the name of the Father, and of the Son, and of the Holy Spirit.

MATTHEW 28:19

My Church

"Yum, what's that smell?" Jamie asked.

"I'm making a casserole. Some of the church ladies are taking dinner over to the Smiths. You know Mrs. Smith has been sick." Mom answered.

"When somebody at church has a problem, everybody kind of helps out, don't they?" Jamie asked.

"Yes, the Bible tells us to do that. We are to help and encourage each other. We care about each other, too." Mom said.

"That's really nice," Jamie said.

How do your church people show they care about each other?

How can you show that you care about others?

Dear God,
Thank you for my church. Thank you for how we care for each other and help each other. Amen.

See how good and pleasant it is when brothers and sisters live together in harmony!

PSALM 133:1

What Is Love?

Sunday
Love Is Kind & Patient

1 CORINTHIANS 13:4

Would you be happy if you had a lot of money? Would you be happy if you could speak any language in the world? If you knew everything that was going to happen in the future would you be happy? If you gave everything you owned to poor people, would that make you happy?

The Bible says that love is the most important thing. Nothing else will make you happy, if you don't love others. The love that God wants you to have for others is kind and patient. When you have this love you are not jealous of others. You don't brag about what you have or who you are.

What makes you happy? When have you been kind to someone?

Dear God,
Thank you for your example of real love. Help me be patient and kind to my friends. Amen.

If we love each other, God lives in us, and his love has reached its goal in us.   1 JOHN 4:12

Monday

Love Is Not Rude or Selfish

1 CORINTHIANS 13:5

best for other people.

Do you enjoy being with someone who is mean to you or someone who is selfish? How do you feel when a friend hurts you? Would a person who loves with God's love act like that?

The Bible says when you love with God's love you will not be rude to your friends. You will not try to make others look bad so that you will look good. You will not be selfish, but will do what is

When has someone been mean to you?

When have you acted selfishly?

Dear God,
Thank you for my friends who treat me kindly and share with me. Help me to love my friends with your kind of love. Amen.

People should be concerned about others and not just about themselves.   1 CORINTHIANS 10:24

278

No Anger or Grudges

1 Corinthians 13:5

Have you ever been playing with a friend and gotten into an argument and your friend starts talking about something wrong you did a long time ago? Or have you ever had a friend who got angry so easily that you had to be careful with every word you said to them?

Loving with God's love means having the patience to hold your temper. It means not getting angry over every little thing. A person who loves like God doesn't keep track of wrong things done to them. That person will forgive and forget.

Who do you know that does not get angry easily?

When have you been able to be patient and hold your temper?

Dear God,
These are hard things to do. It's so easy to get angry and it's easy to hold grudges against some people. Help me to be kinder and more loving so I don't do these things. Amen.

Above all, love each other warmly, because love covers many sins.   1 Peter 4:8

Wednesday

Rejoices in Truth

1 CORINTHIANS 13:6

Do you have a brother or sister? Have you ever been secretly happy when he or she got in trouble with your parents? When you love like God wants you to you will not feel happy when someone gets in trouble. Especially if that person did not do anything wrong.

The love that God gives makes you happy when everyone knows the truth and everyone is judged by the truth. Having God's love makes you want everyone to be treated fairly.

When have you been secretly happy that someone got in trouble?

When have you been glad that you were treated fairly?

Dear God,
Thank you that you always treat everyone fairly. Help me to be happy when everyone is treated fairly. Amen.

To live in love is what we were told to do, and you have heard this from the beginning.

2 JOHN 6

When have you been

Love Protects

1 CORINTHIANS 13:7

When you are working hard to learn something new, doesn't it feel good to know someone believes you can do it? It is comforting to know that no matter what happens, your friend will stand up for you and be loyal to you.

When you love with God's love you will do whatever you can to protect your friends and be loyal to them. If someone is saying bad things about your friend, you will not join in. You will tell them to stop talking about your friend. You will always be strong when it comes to defending your friend.

When has a friend been loyal to you?

When have you stood up for a friend?

Dear God,
That's the kind of friend I want to have. Help me to be a loyal friend who will always stand up for my friends. Amen.

What matters is a faith that expresses itself through love.

GALATIANS 5:6

Love Never Fails

1 CORINTHIANS 13:8

Some people place a lot of importance on the abilities God gave them. They think that being able to teach is very important. Some think that speaking in many languages makes them special. Some think that having great wisdom and understanding is the most important.

But the Bible says that all the gifts we have been given and the abilities we have will be gone someday. The only thing that stays forever is love. Love will go on and on for all time.

Who are some people you love?

How long does God's love last?

Dear God,
Thank you for people who love me. Life is nicer because I am loved. Help me to love others with the kind of love 1 Corinthians 13 talks about. Amen.

I may speak in the languages of humans and of angels. But if I don't have love, . . . I am nothing.

1 CORINTHIANS 13:1-2

Jamie Shows Love

"Quentin is a sissy! Quentin is a sissy!" sang two boys at the park. They were swinging from the highest bar on the jungle gym. They had challenged Jamie and Quentin to swing from that bar too. Jamie took a deep breath and did it. Now Quentin had tried to get his courage up. But the bar was too high and he was scared.

"Come on Jamie, let's leave the sissy to play with the baby toys," said one of the boys. They walked away, expecting Jamie to join them.

"No thanks," Jamie said quietly. "I don't think Quentin is a baby. I'm going to stay here with him."

How did Jamie show love to Quentin?

How do you think Quentin felt about Jamie?

Dear God,
It would be hard to stand up for a friend when others are being mean. Help me to love with your love, so I can be a loyal friend. Amen.

Love never stops being patient, never stops believing, never stops hoping, never gives up.

1 CORINTHIANS 13:7

Living for Christ

Deny Yourself

LUKE 9:23

Is Jesus important to you? Have you asked him to come live in your heart? That means you are a Christian, a child of God. Now you will want to please God.

One way you show you are living for him is by giving up selfish interests and desires. Now you do what God wants you to do. That should be easy because you know God only wants what is best for you. Every day you decide if you will do what God wants or what you want to do.

When have you decided to do what God wants?

How do you know how God wants you to live?

Dear God,
Thank you for wanting what is best for me. Help me to stay close to you and talk to you every day, so I will know what you want for me. Amen.

Those who serve me must follow me. JOHN 12:26

Reading the Bible

JOHN 8:31-32; 2 JOHN 9

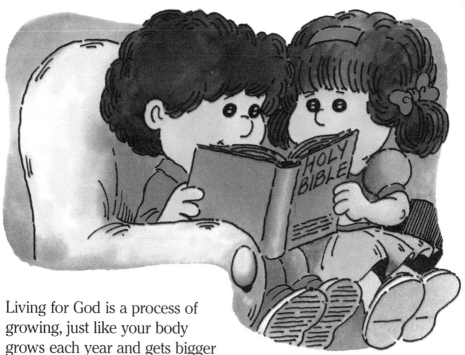

Living for God is a process of growing, just like your body grows each year and gets bigger and taller. You will grow into a better Christian as you learn more about how God wants you to live.

How do you learn more about how God wants you to live? By reading the Bible. It is God's letter to you. It tells you what God is like and what his hopes and dreams are for you. If you live without reading the Bible, you will not know how to please God.

What Bible verse do you know that tells some way God wants you to live?

Do you read or hear the Bible read every day?

Dear God,
Thank you for the Bible. It makes me feel special to think of it as a letter from you. Amen.

I have kept my feet from walking on any evil path in order to obey your word. PSALM 119:101

Prayer

MATTHEW 7:7; JOHN 14:13-14, 15:7

Do you have a good friend with whom you enjoy talking? What do you talk about? Can you ask your friend to help you or to do things for you?

You can talk to God too. He wants you to talk to him all the time. Jesus said you can ask him for anything and he will do it. It's OK to tell him what is important to you. Keep reading the Bible and talking to God and you will get to know him better. You will learn to live the way he wants you to. Then the things that you ask him to do will be things that he wants to do for you.

When do you talk to God?

What are some things you have prayed for?

Dear God,
Thank you for listening to and answering prayer. Thank you for caring about what is important to me. Amen.

If you ask me for anything in my name, I will do it.   JOHN 14:14

Loving Others

JOHN 13:34-35; 1 JOHN 4:11-21

You can show that you love God by the way you treat other people. A person who says he loves God but is mean and hateful to the people around him is showing that he doesn't truly love God.

Showing love for your family and friends is a good way to show God's love to them. When people who do not know God see Christians fighting and arguing, they may become confused about God's love. God's love showing through you could be more powerful than any sermon.

How can you show love to others?

What do you think when you see people arguing and fighting?

Dear God,
I want to show everyone how much you love them and me. Let your love show through me.
Amen.

The person who loves God must also love other believers.

1 JOHN 4:21

287

Bearing Fruit

JOHN 15:5, 8, 16

An apple tree growing in your yard may have many jobs. It provides shade, and it looks nice. But the main thing the apple tree should do is grow apples. When the tree does not do that, it is not doing it's main job.

As a Christian, you have a job to do too. You should be busy telling other people about God. You should be showing others how much God loves them. If you love God, you will be busy doing these things and he will help you. That is the "fruit" which shows God you love him.

Whom have you shown God's love to?

What "fruit" have you grown for God?

Dear God,
Help me be productive for you.
Help me be brave enough to tell
my friends and family members
about your love. Amen.

You honor my Father when you show that you are my disciples by bearing a lot of fruit.

JOHN 15:8

Working Together

1 CORINTHIANS 12:12-31

Look at your body. Do you think your hand is more important than your knee? Is your eye better than your big toe? That is silly, isn't it? Every part of your body is needed so that it works the way it is supposed to.

That is true of God's family too. No one person is more important than anyone else. No one job is more important. Everyone must work together, doing whatever job God has given them to do. Then the message of God's love will be spread all over the world.

Everyone will have a chance to hear about his love.

What job can you do for God?

Have you ever felt that your job wasn't important?

Dear God,
Thank you that I am important in your work. Thank you for giving me a job to do. Amen.

So God put each and every part of the body together as he wanted it.

1 CORINTHIANS 12:18

When I Grow Up

Jamie and his friends were playing in his sandbox and talking together. "When I grow up I'm going to be a famous baseball player," Tommy announced. "I'm gonna be able to hit the baseball harder than anyone ever has."

"Well, when I grow up, I'm gonna be an astronaut and fly spaceships in outer space," said Billy. "Maybe I'll find a planet that no one even knows is out there yet. What are you going to do, Jamie?"

"I don't know yet," Jamie answered. "I want to do whatever God says. Maybe he will want me to be a missionary. Or build big buildings. Or work on a computer like my dad. I'll do whatever he tells me to do."

How can you tell Jamie loves God?

Do you think his friends know he loves God?

Dear God,
Lead me every day. Show me
what you want me to do and
how I can live for you. Amen.

A person may plan his own journey, but the LORD directs his steps.

PROVERBS 16:9

Sunday
Abraham's Special Message

GENESIS 18:1-15

God has special workers that sometimes help him. They are angels. They help God take care of his people, deliver messages to God's people, and protect us.

God had an important message to give Abraham and Sarah. He wanted them to know they were going to have a baby. They had been waiting a long time for this good news.

God sent three angels to Abraham's home. They ate with him. Then they gave him the message from God! "By this time next year, you will have a baby." Abraham and Sarah were very happy.

Who are God's helpers? What are two things they do to help him?

Dear God,
Those three angels must have been happy to bring that news to Abraham. Thank you for good news. Amen.

The son of the slave woman was conceived in a natural way, but the son of the free woman was conceived through a promise made to Abraham.   GALATIANS 4:23

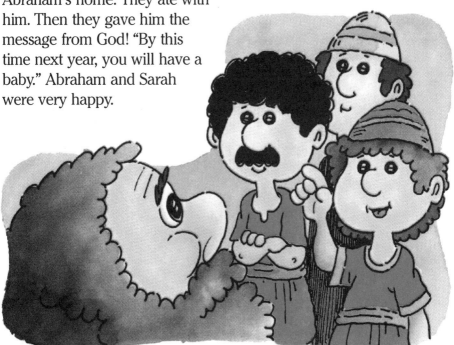

Lot Is Saved

GENESIS 19:1-3, 15-25

Lot lived in a bad city. The people in Sodom did not love God. They did mean things to each other and it was a dangerous place to be. God was tired of the way people in Sodom lived, so he decided to destroy the whole city. But, he wanted Lot to be safe, because Lot loved him. So God sent two angels to tell Lot to get out of Sodom.

When Lot didn't leave right away, the angels grabbed him and his family by the hands and pulled them out of town. They were just in time. Right after they left, fire fell down from heaven and covered the whole city.

Did the angels do the job God wanted them to do?

How can you see God loves his people from this story?

Dear God,
Thank you for sending the angels to save Lot. I know you will take care of me too. Amen.

But whoever listens to me will live without worry and will be free from the dread of disaster.

PROVERBS 1:33

Balaam's Donkey

NUMBERS 22:21-35

A bad king wanted God's people to leave his land because he was afraid of them. So he offered Balaam a lot of money to go and put a curse on them.

God didn't want Balaam to do anything that would hurt his people. So as Balaam was traveling to the king, God sent an angel to block the road in front of Balaam's donkey. The donkey could see the angel, but Balaam couldn't. When the donkey saw it, he went off the road. Balaam hit the donkey to get it back on the road. This happened three times. Finally, God let Balaam see the angel too. The angel said, "Why are you hitting your donkey? He saved your life. I would have killed you to stop you." Now Balaam knew he should obey God.

How did the angel protect Balaam?

How did the donkey protect Balaam?

Dear God,
Thank you for trying to stop me when I am not obeying you. I have not seen an angel, but I know you are there helping me. Amen.

The LORD is a stronghold for the oppressed, a stronghold in times of trouble. PSALM 9:9

293

Wednesday

Baby Announcement

JUDGES 13:2-25

Manoah and his wife did not have any children. One day God sent an angel to visit Manoah's wife. The angel said, "You will have a baby boy. Don't ever cut the baby's hair because he will be a Nazirite." That is a person who serves God for his whole life.

The lady hurried to tell her husband the good news. Manoah went with her to talk to the angel and he was told the same things. But Manoah and his wife were not sure that it was an angel talking to them. Then Manoah offered a burnt offering to God. While it was burning, the angel went up to heaven in the flame. Then

Manoah and his wife knew it was an angel who had brought them the good news.

How do you think Manoah and his wife felt about the news?

How did the angel leave them?

Dear God,
Babies are always happy news.
Thank you for making special announcements in such special ways! Amen.

So the woman had a son and named him Samson. The boy grew up, and the LORD blessed him.   JUDGES 13:24

294

Food for Elijah

1 KINGS 19:3-9

Elijah was sad and tired. He kept trying to do work for the Lord but nothing was going right. Now Elijah had a powerful king and queen angry with him. He ran away and hid in the desert. Elijah sat down under a tree and prayed that God would let him die. Then he fell asleep.

Suddenly an angel woke Elijah and said, "Get up and eat." There was food and water for him. Elijah ate and drank, then fell back asleep.

The angel came again with more food and water. So Elijah ate and drank again. He felt better and continued on his journey.

Why was Elijah so sad?

What did God know that Elijah needed?

Dear God,
Thank you for knowing me so well. You know just what I need to make me feel better. And, you always send it to me. Amen.

If any of you are having trouble, pray.   JAMES 5:13

295

Daniel and the Lions

DANIEL 6

Daniel loved God. He prayed to God every day and served God. Some men did not like Daniel. They wanted to get him in trouble. They got the king to make a law that people could only pray to the king. Then they turned Daniel in when he prayed to God.

Because Daniel didn't pray to the king, he was going to be punished by being thrown into a den of hungry lions. The king did not want to do this to a good man like Daniel, but he had to obey the law. Daniel was put in with the lions.

The next morning the king hurried to see if God protected Daniel. He did! God sent an angel to keep the lions' mouths closed. Now the king told everyone to praise Daniel's God.

Why was Daniel in trouble?
How did God protect Daniel?

Dear God,
Daniel did not do anything wrong, so he should not have been in trouble. Thank you for protecting him. Amen.

God is our refuge and strength, an ever-present help in times of trouble.　　PSALM 46:1

Jamie's Angel

"Mom, does God still send angels to help us like he did in the Bible stories?" Jamie asked.

"Yes, I think he does. But, we may not always know an angel has helped us." Mom said.

Just then Dad came into the room. "Jamie, remember when you got lost from us at the zoo? We looked everywhere for you. A lady found you and took you to the guard's office? That lady may have been an angel.

"Angels can look just like people, so we may not know when God has sent an angel to help us. We can just be thankful that he takes care of us every day."

Do you think Jamie is thankful for God's care?

When has God taken care of you in a special way?

Dear God,
Thank you for watching over me and taking care of me. Amen.

In the fear of the LORD there is strong confidence, and his children will have a place of refuge.

PROVERBS 14:26

More Angel Stories

A Very Hot Furnace

DANIEL 3:1-30

God protected three friends when they got in trouble for worshiping him. Shadrach, Meshach, and Abednego would not bow down and worship a big statue of the king of their land. They loved God and would only worship him. The king was very angry so he had the three friends thrown into a blazing hot furnace.

God sent an angel to protect the three friends. The four of them walked around in the fire and were not hurt at all. They didn't even smell like smoke when the king brought them out of the fire!

Why were the three friends in trouble?

How badly were the three friends hurt?

Dear God,
People should not get in trouble for worshiping you. Thank you for protecting Shadrach, Meshach, and Abednego. Amen.

Praise God . . . . He sent his angel and saved his servants.

DANIEL 3:28

298

An Announcement to Mary

Luke 1:26-38

Mary loved God. She lived her life in a way that made God very happy. God loved Mary, too, and he had a special job for her to do. God sent an angel to tell Mary. The angel said Mary was going to have a baby. God had chosen Mary to be the mother of Jesus, God's very own Son.

Jesus was coming to earth to save people from sin. God knew that Mary would do a good job of taking care of Jesus and helping him grow up safely. Mary was very happy to do this job for God.

Why did God choose Mary to be Jesus' mother?

Why did Jesus come to earth?

Dear God,
That is the best news ever! Thank you that Jesus came and thank you for telling Mary the good news in such a special way!
Amen.

You will . . . give birth to a son, and name him Jesus.   Luke 1:31

Announcement to the Shepherds

LUKE 2:8-14

A group of shepherds were out in the field watching their flocks of sheep. Suddenly the night sky was filled with light. An angel appeared to the shepherds with a special announcement. The shepherds were frightened. But the angel said, "Do not be afraid. I have good news for you. A Savior has been born to you tonight in the village of Bethlehem. He is Christ the Lord." Then more angels joined the first angel and they all sang praises to God.

When the angels were gone, the shepherds hurried to Bethlehem to see the newborn baby.

Were the shepherds surprised to see the angel?

What was the angel's good news?

Dear God,
What a special way to make an announcement! Thank you for the good news of Jesus' birth! Amen.

Glory to God in the highest heaven, and on earth peace to those who have his good will!

LUKE 2:14

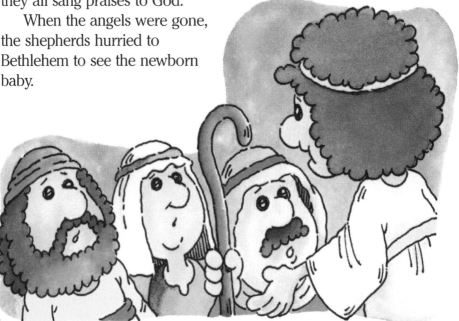

300

Angels in Joseph's Dream

MATTHEW 1:20; 2:13, 19

Joseph was visited by angels at least three times. The first time an angel came to tell him that he should not be afraid to take Mary as his wife. The angel told him the baby she was going to have was the Son of God.

The second time an angel came to warn Joseph that baby Jesus was in danger because a bad king wanted to kill him. The message was to take Mary and the baby and go to another country.

Then when that bad king died an angel came to say it was safe for Joseph, Mary and Jesus to return to their own country.

How did God protect Jesus?

How has God protected you?

Dear God,
I'm glad you know everything that is going to happen to me, like you did with Jesus. Thank you for protecting him and for protecting me. Amen.

I know whom I trust. I'm convinced that he is able to protect what he had entrusted to me until that day   2 TIMOTHY 1:12

Peter and John in Prison

ACTS 5:17-20

Peter and John worked together serving God. They preached and taught about his love to many people. God made them able to do miracles so they healed sick people. Soon people were coming from far away to hear them teach. Many people brought their sick friends and relatives, hoping Peter and John could heal them.

Some of the church leaders were jealous of Peter and John's popularity. So they had them arrested and put in jail. But during the night, God sent an angel to open the jail doors and set Peter and John free. The angel told them to go to the temple courts and preach about God's love.

Why were the church leaders jealous of Peter and John?

What did the angel tell Peter and John to do?

Dear God,
Thank you that no evil power can stop your Word. Thank you for freeing Peter and John and telling them to keep on preaching. Amen.

Every day in the temple courtyard and from house to house, they refused to stop teaching and telling the Good News that Jesus is the Christ.

ACTS 5:42

Peter in Prison

ACTS 12:1-11

Peter was in trouble because he was ordered to stop talking about Jesus. But, he kept on preaching. So now he was in prison, chained between two guards. Sixteen more soldiers guarded the prison.

Peter's friends were praying for his safety. God wanted Peter to be safe so he sent an angel to him. The angel released Peter's chains and led him out of the prison. They walked past all the guards and through the locked prison doors.

When they got out to the street, the angel disappeared. Peter hurried to tell his friends that God had saved him.

Why was Peter in prison? How do you know God wanted Peter to be safe?

Dear God,
Thank you for helping Peter.
Thank you for watching over me
and helping me. Amen.

The Lord . . . knows how to rescue godly people when they are tested.   2 PETER 2:9

Saturday

The Announcement

Jamie sat cross-legged on the floor watching television while he played with his blocks. Suddenly he heard a loud "beep-beep-beep" coming from the TV. He looked up and saw words going across the bottom of the screen. He called Dad to read the words.

"The words are a warning that there may be a bad thunderstorm coming," Dad explained. "They are warning people to stay inside and be ready."

"Oh, angel words," Jamie said. "Like when the angel warned Joseph to protect baby Jesus. I guess before TV God made announcements with angels."

Dad smiled, "I don't think the TV changed God's way of making announcements."

What are some ways God warns you of danger?
What is your favorite angel story?

Dear God,
Thank you for doing whatever you need to do to take care of me. I'm glad you and your angels are always around me. Amen.

We must fear the LORD, the Most High. He is the great king of the whole earth.

PSALM 47:2

Prayer

Sunday

The Way Not to Pray

MATTHEW 6:5-8

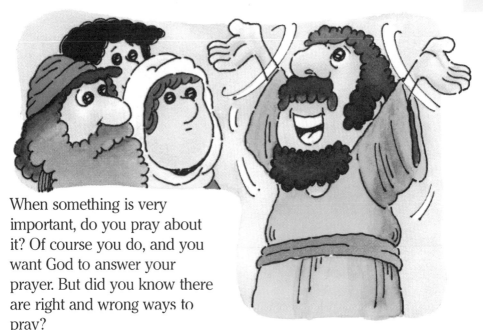

When something is very important, do you pray about it? Of course you do, and you want God to answer your prayer. But did you know there are right and wrong ways to pray?

Jesus wanted his followers to know the right way to pray. He told them not to pray just to show off to other people. Some people only pray loudly and in front of people so everyone can hear them. They are not really talking to God, they are showing off. Jesus said that when you really want God to listen, go into your closet and pray quietly, so no one but God can hear you.

Why would someone pray to show off?

Where is a quiet place you can go to pray?

Dear God,
I didn't know there were right and wrong ways to pray. Help me to pray for the right reasons and not to show off. Amen.

When you pray, go to your room and close the door. Pray privately to your Father who is with you. Your Father sees what you do in private. He will reward you.

MATTHEW 6:6

The Lord's Prayer

MATTHEW 6:9-13

When Jesus taught his followers, he didn't just tell them what they should not do. He gave them examples of the right way to do things. So, when Jesus was teaching them how to pray, he gave them an example of the right way to pray.

Jesus' example of prayer is now called The Lord's Prayer. It showed us that when we pray, we should start with praising God for who he is. Then ask that God's will be done on earth. Next we should ask God to forgive our sins and help us to forgive others. We should ask God to keep us from being tempted to do wrong and to protect us from Satan.

Say the Lord's Prayer with an adult.
What would you like to praise God for?

Dear God,
Thank you for a model prayer. It is easier to learn when there is a sample. Thank you for thinking of everything! Amen.

Your Father knows what you need before you ask him.

MATTHEW 6:8

Praise God!

EPHESIANS 1:3-15; HEBREWS 13:15

There is so much about God that we can praise! He likes to hear our praise, it shows that we know how wonderful he is and how much he has done for us. The Bible tells us to praise God all the time. Tell him you know how wonderful he is.

God can be praised because he created everything. He chose us to be his children before we were even born! We can be Christians because Jesus was willing to die for our sins. Praise him for the gift of the Holy Spirit who lives in us, helping us understand what God is like and how we can be more like him.

How do you feel when a friend says something nice about you?

Praise God for all the wonderful things he has done for you.

Dear God,
Praise God for making the world. Praise him for my family and my church. Praise him for the gift of Jesus who makes life with God possible. Amen.

We should always bring God our sacrifices through Jesus.

HEBREWS 13:15

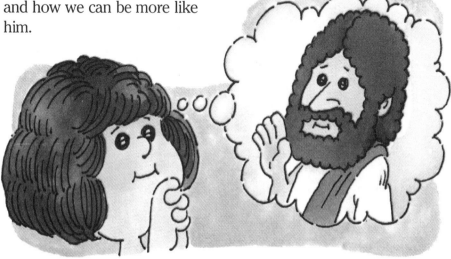

307

Give Thanks!

MARK 6:41; ROMANS 7:25; EPHESIANS 5:4; PHILIPPIANS 1:3

When someone does something nice for you, do you say thank you? It is good to thank God for the things he does for you, too. It can be easy to get caught up in only asking God to do this or that. But, the Bible has many examples of thanksgiving. The people in the Bible knew that it was important to thank God for all he had given them. There are prayers of thanks for people who are strong in their faith. There are prayers of thanks for food. Prayer of thanks for helping stop sin.

There is so much to thank God for, we should be thanking him every minute of every day.

How many things can you list that God has given you?

How often do you thank him for those things?

Dear God,
Thank you, thank you, thank you! Everything I am and everything I have is a gift from you. Thank you. Amen.

You received Christ Jesus the Lord, so continue to live as Christ's people.

COLOSSIANS 2:6

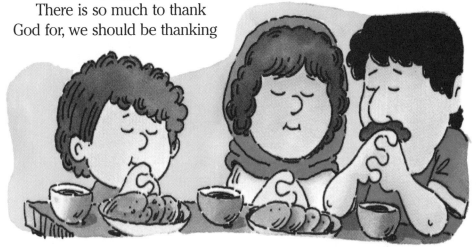

Confession Is Good for the Soul

LUKE 15:21; 1 JOHN 1:9

If you break your mother's favorite lamp, do not blame a younger brother or sister. When you do something wrong, admit it, to the person you wronged and to God.

This is another kind of prayer. It is called a prayer of confession. Jesus gave an example of confession in the story of the boy who asked his father for money, then left home and spent all the money. He came back to his father and admitted he had done wrong. His father forgave him.

When we confess to God that we have done wrong things, he promises to forgive us and to remember that Jesus' death washed away all our sins.

Why does God forgive us?

What do you need to confess to God?

Dear God,
I do wrong things and I am sorry for them. Please forgive me and help me to do right things. Amen.

Wash me and I will be whiter than snow. PSALM 51:7

Asking for What You Want

MATTHEW 7:7-8; PHILIPPIANS 4:6; JAMES 1:5-8

What kinds of things do you pray for? Are there things you want to ask God to do for you or someone else? That is just fine with God. The Bible says that if you want God to do something for you or for someone else, ask him. In fact, the Bible says that some people do not have what they need because they do not ask him.

But when you ask him, believe that he will answer you. A person who asks God for something, but does not believe he will answer, will not get an answer.

When have you prayed for something, but not really believed God would answer?

What is something very important you would like God to do for you now?

*Dear God,
Sometimes it is hard to believe you will answer my prayers. You have a whole world to take care of. Thank you for caring about me. Amen.*

Never worry about anything. But in every situation let God know what you need in prayers and requests while giving thanks.

PHILIPPIANS 4:6

"Now I Lay Me . . ."

"NowIlaymedowntosleep . . ." Jamie began praying, as fast has his tongue could spit out the words.

"Whoa, Jamie. You aren't even thinking about what you are asking God to do," Dad interrupted. "Prayer is a special time to talk to God and tell him what is important to you. Don't just say words you have learned. Think about what you are saying to him."

"I'm sorry," Jamie said. Then he began a real prayer, "Dear God, Thank you for Mom and Dad. . ."

When have you prayed without thinking about the words you were saying?

Talk to God now and tell him something that is important to you.

Dear God,
I'm sorry that I sometimes say words to you without thinking about what I am praying. Please forgive me. Thank you. Amen.

You don't have the things you want, because you don't ask for them.

JAMES 4:2

311

Sharing the Good News

The Example of Paul

ACTS 18

Before Paul became a Christian, he spent all his energy trying to stop people from talking about God. But, when Jesus called Paul, everything changed. After Paul found out how much Jesus loved him, he became a Christian. Then he wanted everyone to know about God's love.

Paul spent the rest of his life preaching and teaching about God's love. Many times people got angry at Paul because of his excitement in preaching God's love. Sometimes he was even put in prison. But Paul never stopped sharing the Good News.

Why did Paul change?
When things got tough,
did Paul give up?

Dear God,
Thank you for Paul's example.
He wanted everyone to know
about you. He never stopped
telling others about you.
Help me to have that kind of
excitement for you. Amen.

The prize for a life that has God's approval is now waiting for me. The Lord, who is a fair judge, will give me the prize on that day.

2 TIMOTHY 4:8

Barnabas

Acts 4:36-37; 11:22-26

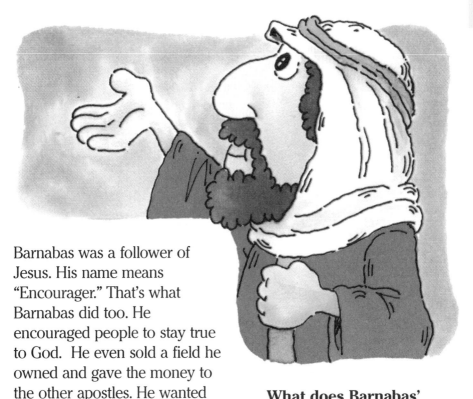

Barnabas was a follower of Jesus. His name means "Encourager." That's what Barnabas did too. He encouraged people to stay true to God. He even sold a field he owned and gave the money to the other apostles. He wanted to help everyone.

Barnabas was a good man with a lot of faith in God. Many people believed in God because of Barnabas.

But he didn't have to work by himself, either. One time he and Paul taught the people in Antioch. They stayed for a whole year and taught the people about Jesus and his love for them.

What does Barnabas' name mean?

How did Barnabas encourage people?

Dear God,
Help me be an encourager. Help me encourage people to stay close to you and learn more about you. Amen.

Barnabas was a dependable man, and he was full of the Holy Spirit and faith.   Acts 11:24

313

Tuesday

Priscilla and Aquila

ACTS 18:24-28; ROMANS 16:3-5

Priscilla and Aquila were a team. They were husband and wife and they both loved God. They worked together to tell others about him. Paul met them on one of his trips and he saw their great faith. So he asked them to travel with him on some of his missionary trips. There was even a church that met in Priscilla and Aquila's home.

One time Priscilla and Aquila heard a man named Apollos preaching about God. They saw that he was excited about what he was teaching. But, he didn't know the whole story of what Jesus had done. So, Priscilla and Aquila told him the rest of the story. Apollos was glad to hear what they told him.

Name one way Priscilla and Aquila served God.

Who could you work with as a team?

Dear God,
I'm glad I can know the whole story of what Jesus did for me. Thank you for the people who have taught me about you. Amen.

May God, who gives you this endurance and encouragement, allow you to live in harmony with each other by following the example of Christ Jesus. Then, having the same goal, you will praise the God and Father of our Lord Jesus Christ.   ROMANS 15:5-6

Timothy

1 Cor. 4:17; 1 Timothy 4:11-12; 2 Timothy 1:5

Timothy was a young man when he started serving God. His mother and grandmother taught him about God from the time he was a little boy. Paul spent time with Timothy and taught him more and more about God. Timothy traveled with Paul on some of his missionary trips. Paul even sent Timothy to some of the churches he had started to see how they were doing.

Paul encouraged Timothy to keep serving God even though he was young. No one should think less of Timothy because of his youth. In fact, Paul said Timothy could be an example to other believers by the way he lived.

How can you serve God as a young person?
How can you tell that Timothy loved God?

Dear God,
It is good to know that there are ways for young people to serve you. Help me to find my way. Amen.

Don't let anyone look down on you for being young. Instead, make your speech, behavior, love, faith, and purity an example for other believers.

1 Timothy 4:12

Peter

Acts 2:14-41

Peter was a fisherman when he was called to follow Jesus. Peter left his boat and nets and went with Jesus. Peter enjoyed preaching about Jesus' love.

One time when Peter was explaining the message of Jesus' love, some men started to make fun of the Christians because they acted different from other people. Peter explained an Old Testament scripture to them. Then he told them that the believers were acting this way because the Holy Spirit had been given to them. Peter told the men to turn away from their sin so they could receive the Holy Spirit too.

Was Peter shy?
How can you tell that
Peter knew the Bible?

Dear God,
Help me to know your word so that I can explain it and use it to tell others about you. Amen.

Whoever calls on the name of the Lord will be saved.

Acts 2:21

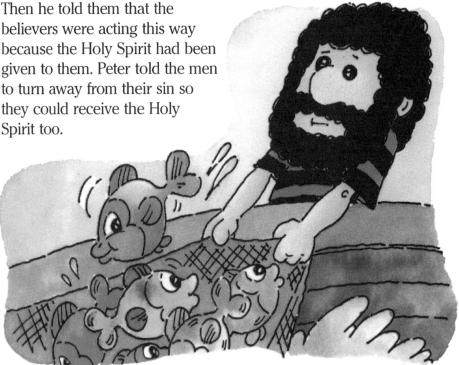

Silas

Acts 16:16-34; 1 Peter 5:12

Silas spent much of his life telling people about Jesus. It wasn't always easy. One time he was traveling with Paul. They made some people angry by healing a girl who was possessed by a demon. So the people put them in jail.

During the night a big earthquake shook the jail so hard that the doors fell open. Paul and Silas and the other prisoners could have escaped, but they didn't. When the jailer saw they had stayed, he asked them how he could be saved. Soon the jailer and his whole family were Christians.

Why were Paul and Silas put in jail?

Why did the jailer want to know how to be saved?

Dear God,
I love hearing about how your Word is shared. Thank you for making Paul and Silas stay in the jail when they could have left. If they can be brave for you, I can too. Amen.

Believe in the Lord Jesus, and you and your family will be saved. Acts 16:31

317

Jamie Shares the Good News

Jamie and Tommy were playing in the sandbox. Tommy was Jamie's very best friend. They always had a lot of fun together. But today Tommy was not much fun. He was too sad. Tommy's grandpa was very sick and Tommy was worried about him.

"Tommy, would you like for me to say a prayer that your grandpa would get better?" Jamie asked.

"I guess so. But I'm not sure it will do any good," Tommy said sadly.

"Sure it will, God loves you and your grandpa, don't you know that?" Jamie answered. "Let me tell you about everything God has done for you. You won't believe how much he loves you!"

How did Jamie tell his friend about the Good News?

To whom can you tell the Good News?

Dear God,
I have some really good friends and I want them to know about your love. Help me find the right words to tell them. Amen.

A prayer offered in faith will save a sick person, and the Lord will heal him.

JAMES 5:15

Learning God's Word

Sunday

Hearing the Word

LUKE 11:28; ROMANS 10:17; 1 PETER 2:2-3

Do you have a favorite book that you ask your mom or dad to read you over and over? Can you say the words in the book by heart because you have heard it so much? That is the way you can learn what the Bible says. If someone reads it to you over and over you will learn to know the words, just like you do that favorite book. You can hear God's Word at Sunday School and Church and also at home.

Hearing God's Word read to you not only helps you learn it; it helps his word get into your heart. Then you will want to know more about him. So you will know how God wants you to treat other people and how you should treat him.

What is your favorite book?

How often do you hear the Bible read?

Dear God,
Help me to listen every time your Word is being read. Help me to learn more about you by hearing your Word. Amen.

Blessed are those who hear and obey God's word.

LUKE 11:28

Study God's Word

ACTS 17:11; REVELATION 1:3

Do you know how to say the alphabet? Can you count to twenty? How did you learn to do those things? The best way to learn something, or to understand it, is to study it. That means repeating it or practicing it over and over. That is also how you can learn and understand what is written in the Bible.

If you hear a Bible verse and it doesn't make sense to you, look up other verses about the same subject. Read the entire chapter the verse is in. Ask your family questions. Do everything you can to understand what you are reading. The words in the Bible will change your life.

What part of the Bible have you not understood before?

What can you do to understand the Bible more?

Dear God,
Thank you for giving us the Bible. I know it is important to understand what it says. Help me to study and understand what you want me to know. Amen.

Also take salvation as your helmet and the word of God as the sword that the Spirit supplies.

EPHESIANS 6:17

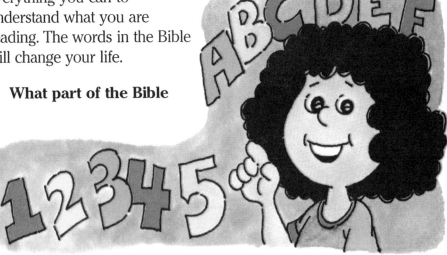

Memorize God's Word

PSALM 119:9, 11

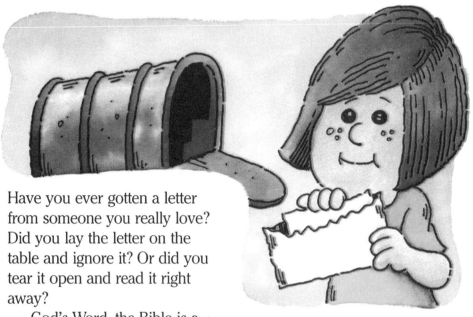

Have you ever gotten a letter from someone you really love? Did you lay the letter on the table and ignore it? Or did you tear it open and read it right away?

God's Word, the Bible is a personal letter to you from God. It will help you with any problem you have. It will tell you how to be a better person and how to live the way God says you should live.

But you do not carry the Bible with you to the playground. If you have a problem and need to know what the Bible says, what do you do?

You can memorize it. When you learn God's Word by heart, it is always with you. Then you can remember it anytime.

How do you memorize something?

What Bible verses have you memorized?

Dear God,
I want to have your Word with me all the time. Help me learn Bible verses that will help me. Amen.

Take to heart these words that I give you today.   DEUTERONOMY 6:6

Think about God's Word

PSALM 1:2-3; PHILIPPIANS 4:8-9

Did you know that what you think about can make a difference in how you act? If you spend lots of time watching TV programs that show violence and bad things, you are not putting good thoughts in your mind.

The Bible says to think about what the Bible says all the time. When you put good things in your mind, it helps you be a better person. Thinking about the Bible is thinking about things that are good and right. It is thinking about what God has done for you and how much he loves

you. That is a good thing to put in your mind!

How much time do you spend watching TV?

How much time do you spend reading the Bible?

Dear God,
What goes in my mind comes out in how I act. Help me to put good things in my mind. Amen.

Blessed are those whose thoughts are pure.   MATTHEW 5:8

Living out God's Word

JAMES 1:22; 2:14-20

Reading God's Word and studying God's Word means nothing if you don't live the way it teaches you to live. Even memorizing God's Word means nothing if it doesn't show in your life.

If you read and memorize God's Word, but are still mean to your brothers and sisters, or show disrespect to your parents, then knowing God's Word doesn't mean anything. Let the Bible change you. Live the way God's Word says to live. You will be happier!

What verse can you think of that says one way to treat others?

When have you obeyed that verse?

Dear God,
Some of my friends may never go to church, but they can see what you are like by how I treat them. Help me to be a good example of your love. Amen.

I will show you my faith by the things I do.   JAMES 2:18

Friday

Sharing God's Word

MATTHEW 28:19-20

If something good happens to you, do you keep it secret and not tell anyone? Of course not! You run to tell your friends. You want them to share your happiness.

There is no better news in the whole world than the news that God loves you and sent Jesus to earth so you can live in heaven someday. Jesus said to tell everyone about him. You can tell your friends about God's love. Tell them how the Bible will help them with any problem they have. Tell them how knowing it will help them to be better happier people.

When have you told a friend about God's love?

What friend could you invite to church to hear about God's love?

Dear God,
Help me be sensitive to my friends. Help me know when is the right time to talk to them about you. Give me the right words to say. Amen.

Go everywhere in the world, and tell everyone the Good News.

MARK 16:15

Jamie Learns God's Word

"Mo-o-o-o-om," Jamie called at the top of his lungs.

"Downstairs, Jamie," Mom answered.

"Mom, my Sunday School teacher wants me to learn a Bible verse every week — by heart!" Jamie said. "I have to learn one for Sunday School tomorrow."

"OK, let's pick a subject. Every week you can learn a verse on that subject. How about starting with God's love? Your first verse can be John 3:16," Mom suggested.

"OK, will you help me learn it?"

"Sure, let's get your Bible," Mom said as she started up the stairs.

What verses have you memorized for Sunday School?

What topic would you like to study?

Dear God,
Help me to take your Word seriously. Help me to put it in my heart where I can always have it with me. Amen.

Your commandments make me wiser than my enemies, because your commandments are always with me.

PSALM 119:98

The Fruit of the Spirit

Sunday
The Gift of the Holy Spirit

MATTHEW 7:16-20; GALATIANS 5:16

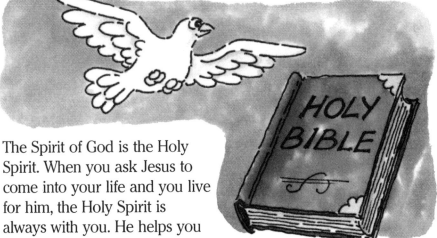

The Spirit of God is the Holy Spirit. When you ask Jesus to come into your life and you live for him, the Holy Spirit is always with you. He helps you change and grow and become the person God wants you to be. He does not make you change, but he is there to help you if you ask him.

God does not judge you by your actions or the work you do for him. But if you are reading the Bible and talking to him every day, it will show in your actions. Jesus talked about a fruit tree that did not grow any fruit. It was still a fruit tree, but it was not doing the job it was supposed to do. A Christian should do the job God gives him, and the Holy Spirit is there to help you do that job.

Does the Holy Spirit make you do things you do not want to do?

What is something about you that has changed since you became a Christian?

Dear God,
The Holy Spirit living in me is hard to understand. But, thank you that he will help me become the person you want me to be. I know you only want what is best for me. Amen.

I pray that your love will keep on growing because of your knowledge and insight.

PHILIPPIANS 1:9

Love and Joy

GALATIANS 5:22

Do you say you are a Christian who loves God? How do you treat the people around you? The fruits of love and joy are very easy to see in your life. It is very hard to pretend you are loving and joyful if you are not.

Jesus said to love others more than yourself and to love others as much as he loves you. You should love Jesus first, others second, and yourself last.

Another fruit of the spirit is a heart that is full of joy. Joy is more than just a smile on your face. It is happiness that comes from your heart and bubbles out. Joy is happiness because of all that God has done for you.

Are you usually a happy person?
When is a time these two fruits could be seen in you?

I have told you this so that you will have my joy in you and that your joy will be complete.

JOHN 15:11

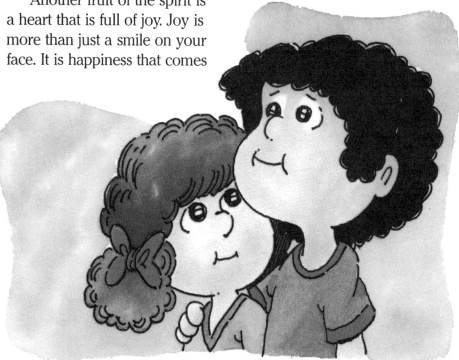

Peace and Patience

GALATIANS 5:22

Do you know someone who is always arguing and complaining? Do you like to be around that person?

Two other fruits that the Holy Spirit can help grow in your life are peace and patience. The Holy Spirit can help you learn to live in peace with those around you. People who do not know God will notice how well you get along with others. They may ask you why you are so peaceful. It will give you a chance to tell them about God.

Being patient means you do not try to hurry God. You take life as it comes and trust him to do what is best for you.

Who do you know that is peaceful and patient?

When have you needed to be more patient?

Dear God,
Peace and patience are not easy!
Help me to let this fruit grow in my life. Then my friends will see how much I love you. Amen.

So let's pursue those things which bring peace and which are good for each other. ROMANS 14:19

Kindness and Goodness

GALATIANS 5:22

An easy way to see the fruit of the Holy Spirit in your life is by kindness. A kind person looks for ways to be nice to other people. A kind person wants to help others any way he can. The kindness that comes from the Holy Spirit is not just for your friends. This is kindness you will show to people who are different from you. People who may be poor; or people that your friends do not like. The Holy Spirit will help you show kindness and goodness to everyone you meet.

How do you feel when someone is kind to you?
Who is someone it is hard for you to be kind to?

Dear God,
Give me kindness so that I can be kind to everyone I meet.
Thank you for the kindness you always have. Amen.

Be kind to each other, sympathetic, forgiving each other as God has forgiven you through Christ. EPHESIANS 4:32

Faithfulness

GALATIANS 5:22

It is easy to be a Christian when you are surrounded by other Christians; when everyone believes the same things and everyone cares about God. But what would happen if none of the people around you cared about God? What if they lived in a way that did not please him? Would you keep living for God? Would you go against the crowd? If you did, you would be faithful to God.

The Holy Spirit will help you live for God, even in hard situations. He will give you the strength to get through hard things.

When has it been hard for you to be faithful to God?

Will you ask God to help you be faithful?

Dear God,
Thank you for all your promises.
Please help me be faithful to you,
no matter what happens. Amen.

The LORD protects faithful people, but he pays back in full those who act arrogantly.

PSALM 31:23

Gentleness and Self-Control

GALATIANS 5:23

How does a mother treat her brand-new baby? She picks the baby up gently and tenderly cradles him in her arms. She rocks him and sings to him softly. Do you show gentleness to people? Do you speak softly and consider their feelings? The Holy Spirit can help you do that.

Self-control is another fruit of the Spirit that helps you control your temper and patience. Having self-control means you do not do things like eating too much or overdoing any activity, even if it is something good.

What did you do today that showed self-control?
When have you been gentle?

Dear God,
Help me listen to what the Holy Spirit tries to teach me. Help me learn to be more like you.
Amen.

Surrender yourself to the LORD, and wait patiently for him.

PSALM 37:7

Saturday

Jamie Learns about Growth

Jamie and Dad were planting their summer garden. Dad had worked all morning preparing the ground. Now he was digging little trenches. Jamie walked along behind him and dropped seeds in the trenches and gently covered them with dirt.

"Jamie, we will keep these seeds watered, and pull out any weeds that grow. Before long we'll have a nice garden and plenty of good vegetables to eat," Dad said. Then he added, "These plants will be fruitful, the same way we can be when the Holy Spirit grows the fruit of the Spirit in us. Remember what we read?"

"Yes, and I remember that the fruits are things like love and joy and peace. They only grow in us when we let the Spirit do his work," Jamie said.

When a plant begins to grow, does it start out big or small?

How do you think the fruit of the Spirit starts out in people?

Dear God,
I want the fruit of the Spirit in me. Help me be a good garden for you! Amen.

But the spiritual nature produces love, joy, peace, patience, kindness, goodness, faithfulness, gentleness, and self-control. There are no rules against things like that.

GALATIANS 5:22-23

Sunday

Paul's First Time Preaching

Acts 9:19-31

Before Paul became a Christian, he hated everyone who believed in God. He tried to stop people from talking about him. Then Paul became a Christian and right away he started preaching. That made all of his old friends mad! They even wanted to kill him. They watched the city gates, planning to grab Paul when he tried to leave town. Paul and his friends knew what they were planning. So, Paul's friends put him in a basket and let him down over the city wall.

Paul went to Jerusalem and continued preaching. Many hard things happened to Paul, but he never stopped talking about God and his love.

Why did Paul's old friends want to kill him?

What made Paul stop preaching?

Dear God,
Give me the courage Paul had.
Help me to never stop talking
about you, no matter what!
Amen.

We know that all things work together for the good of those who love God–those whom he has called according to his plan.

Romans 8:28

To Lystra

ACTS 14:8-18

Paul and Barnabas were in Lystra when they saw a crippled man. The man listened carefully to what Paul taught him. When Paul saw that the man believed, he healed him.

Some of the people who saw what Paul did, started shouting that Paul and Barnabas were gods! The people wanted to worship them. Paul told them they were wrong!

Paul and Barnabas were not gods, they were just men who were teaching the Good News of Jesus Christ. Paul told the people they should not worship men, but worship the one true God.

Why did the people want to worship Paul and Barnabas?

What did Paul say about what the people wanted to do?

Dear God,
I pray that I will never let some person be so important that I want to worship him. Help me to save that spot for you. Amen.

Never make your own carved idols or statues that represent any creature in the sky, on the earth, or in the water. EXODUS 20:4

Lydia's Conversion
Acts 16:11-15

Paul traveled to many cities preaching the good news. In one city, a woman named Lydia heard his teaching. She was with a group of women on a river bank. Lydia knew about God, she even worshiped him, but she wasn't really a believer.

But, when Lydia heard Paul speak, God opened her heart and she understood what he was saying. Lydia believed that day. Right away she invited Paul and his friends to come and stay at her home.

Your friends may not believe when you tell them about God, but you may plant a seed that someday will help them believe.

Why wasn't Lydia a believer before she heard Paul?

What did Lydia do as soon as she believed?

Dear God,
Just hearing about you doesn't make someone a Christian, but it is a beginning. Thank you for sending people like Paul to keep telling people about you. Maybe, like Lydia, my friends will soon believe. Amen.

She was listening because the Lord made her willing to pay attention to what Paul said.
Acts 16:14

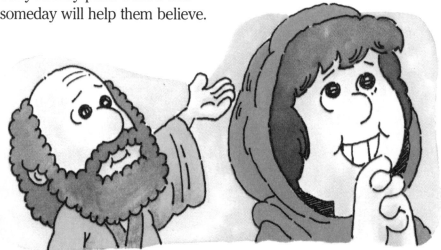

Paul Teaches in Athens

Acts 17:16-34

Paul was in Athens, a city full of people who worshiped many gods that they had made into gold and silver idols. Paul was upset to find an altar that was *To an Unknown God.* So he began teaching the people about the real God.

He told them how God made the world and everything in it. God does not live in a temple that people have built and human hands do not control him. They should not think that a piece of silver or gold can represent God. God will judge everyone for how they live, so they should turn away from their sin and love God.

Some people wanted to hear more about God, but some people just made fun of Paul.

How do you know the people in Athens were religious?

What altar upset Paul the most?

Dear God,
Thank you for sending Paul. He was brave and taught about you any place he went. Give me courage to speak up for you too.
Amen.

He has done this so that they would look for God, somehow reach for him, and find him. In fact, he is never far from any one of us. Acts 17:27

Eutychus

Acts 20:7-12

Have you ever fallen asleep in church? Eutychus did, and it made for quite a story. Eutychus was listening to Paul preach. Paul had so much to tell the people that he preached for a long time. They were in a hot, crowded room and it got to be very late at night. Eutychus was sitting in an open window listening to Paul. But, he got so hot and tired that he went to sleep and fell out the window. His friends ran to check on him, and they found he was dead!

Paul came out and fell down on Eutychus crying, "He's alive!" Then Paul went in and preached all night! Eutychus was alive. Everyone who saw this happen was amazed.

Why did Eutychus fall asleep?

What did Paul do about Eutychus?

Dear God,
Paul had a lot to say! He just kept on preaching after Eutychus' accident. Nothing should stop me from talking about you, either. Amen.

I'm not ashamed of the Good News. It is God's power to save everyone who believes, Jews first and Greeks as well.   Romans 1:16

Timothy

2 TIMOTHY 3:10–4:8

Paul taught Timothy how to work in churches and teach others about God. He sent Timothy to work in some churches where the people were having trouble. Then he wrote letters to Timothy to encourage him. Paul wrote the letter that is now 2 Timothy in our Bibles from prison.

Paul told Timothy to be strong in the Lord, just as Paul had always been. Timothy should keep telling people about Jesus, no matter how hard things might get. Paul reminded Timothy that a reward was waiting in heaven for everyone that kept serving God.

How can you tell that Paul cared about teaching Timothy?
Why should you never stop telling others about God?

Dear God,
Help me be strong like Paul and Timothy. Help me keep talking about you. Amen.

Be ready to spread the word whether or not the time is right. Point out errors, warn people, and encourage them. Be very patient when you teach.   2 TIMOTHY 4:2

Jamie's Hero

"Mom, you should see Dillon's notebook. It is full of Superhero cards. He has every card made, I think," Jamie said. "I want to start a collection like his."

"Aren't Superheros the comic book characters?" Mom asked.

"Yea, they are the greatest!"

"Well, I'm sure they are, but let's see if we can't think of a 'Superhero' from the Bible, someone who didn't let anything get in the way of telling about Jesus," Mom said.

Are comic book characters or Bible people better "Superheroes"?

How can you be like Paul?

Dear God,
Comic books are OK. But I want to live like Paul. Thank you for telling me about him in the Bible. Amen.

I have kept the faith.

2 TIMOTHY 4:7

Old Testament Leaders

Noah Served When Others Didn't

GENESIS 6–8

God was pleased with Noah. Most other people on earth were doing what they wanted to do and paying no attention to God. But, Noah loved God and served him. So when God decided to destroy the world he had made, he saved Noah.

God had Noah build a big boat and put his family on the boat along with every kind of animal on earth. Then God destroyed the world with a big flood, except for the people and animals on the boat.

When the flood was over, God promised he would never do that again. As a sign of his promise he put a rainbow in the sky. Then Noah got off the boat and started life on earth again.

Who was the man who loved God when others didn't?

What is a sign of God's promise that he will not destroy the earth with a flood again?

Dear God,
Thank you for the example of Noah who served you when others didn't. Noah obeyed you and built the big boat, before it even started to rain. Help me be that obedient. Amen.

I will put my rainbow in the clouds to be a sign of my promise to the earth.

GENESIS 9:13

Joash's Good Idea

2 KINGS 11:21–12:16

Joash became king of Judah when he was only 7 years old. He was a good king who loved God. Joash knew that God's temple needed to be fixed up. By the time he was in his twenties, he decided to do something about it.

Joash's plan was to use the money that people gave at the temple. So a special box for offerings was put in the temple. The money was used to pay the men who worked on the temple.

Finally the temple was repaired and it was all paid for by God's people. God was happy with what Joash did.

How old was Joash when he became king?

How were the repairs paid for?

Dear God,
Thank you for the example of Joash. He wasn't very old, but he had a good idea of how to serve God. Amen.

It is God who produces in you the desires and actions that please him.　　PHILIPPIANS 2:13

Joshua Obeys

NUMBERS 27:18-23; JOSHUA 1; 6

Moses led the Israelites for a long time. He loved God and God spoke directly to Moses. But, Moses could not live forever. So God chose Joshua to take over the leadership of the people when Moses died. God promised to be with Joshua, just as he was with Moses.

God helped Joshua do many wonderful things. He stopped the waters of the Jordan River so the people could cross on dry ground. Joshua obeyed God and the walls of the city of Jericho fell down and the Israelites captured the city. Joshua led the Israelites in capturing the whole land that God promised to them.

Why would it be hard to lead after a great leader like Moses?

What things have you done for God?

Dear God,
You and Joshua made a great team. He obeyed you and you helped him do some exciting things! I want to be on your team too. Amen.

The LORD said to Moses' assistant Joshua . . . Be strong and courageous.

JOSHUA 1:1, 6

342

Esther Is Not Afraid

ESTHER 2; 4–5

Esther was a Jewish girl who was in a hard situation. She was chosen to be queen of a king who did not love God. She was given this honor because of her great beauty. But also because God had a job for her to do.

Haman was a bad man who worked for the king. Haman did not like any of the Jews and made plans to have them all killed. But he did not know Queen Esther was Jewish.

Esther had to risk her own life to save the Jews. But she did it! God used her in a special way.

Why was Esther chosen queen?

Would you be as brave as Esther?

Dear God,
I would like to be brave like Esther. She risked her own life to serve you and her people. Give me courage. Amen.

Esther sent this reply back to Mordecai, "Assemble all the Jews in Susa. Fast for me . . . I will go to the king, ... If I die, I die."

ESTHER 4:15, 16

343

David Does Right

1 SAMUEL 17; 19; 26;

David was only a young boy when he was chosen to serve God as the next king of Israel. He loved God and God helped him do many things. David killed a nine foot giant, when the whole Israelite army was afraid of him. David led his army to defeat many of the Israelites enemies.

The people cheered for David, and King Saul became very jealous of him. He even tried to kill him. David did not try to get even with Saul even though he had chances to do so.

Eventually Saul died, and David was made king.

Would you like to be king of a nation?

What would you do if someone was mean to you?

Dear God,
I think I might try to get even with someone who was mean to me. David was very strong to not do that. He must have really wanted to serve you. Thank you for his example. Amen.

The LORD should be praised. I called on him, and I was saved from my enemies.

2 SAMUEL 22:4

Moses Serves God

EXODUS 3

It was obvious from the time Moses was born that God had big plans for him. He saved Moses from being killed as a baby. He had Moses grow up in a palace as the son of an Egyptian princess.

God spoke to Moses from a burning bush and told him to lead the Israelites out of slavery in Egypt. God gave Moses the Ten Commandments from up on a mountaintop. God parted the waters of the Red Sea so the Israelites could escape the Egyptian king. Moses led the Israelites through the wilderness to the edge of the land God had promised to give them.

Why does it seem God had special things for Moses to do?

What is one miracle God did for Moses?

Dear God,
I'm glad you saved Moses from death as a baby. You always protect the people who love you. Thank you for watching over me. Amen.

The LORD is my rock and my fortress and my Savior.

2 SAMUEL 22:2

345

Jamie Understands

"I don't know why we have to read about the things these old people did in Bible times," Jamie moaned. "They lived a long time ago, what do I care what they did?"

"But Jamie, reading about Moses and David and Noah and the others shows us how God has cared for his people for thousands of years. When we see everything he has done, we can believe he will keep doing those kinds of things for us. God takes care of his people." Dad explained. "We can also learn how to live for God by seeing how Bible characters sometimes didn't trust God, and sometimes did trust him. The Old Testament is full of examples of people who lived for God through good and bad times."

Which Bible character do you like to hear about?
What do you learn from that person?

Dear God,
Examples make learning a lot easier. It's easier to understand what you want from me when I see someone else living it. Help me to learn from the examples you have given. Amen.

The LORD will rule as king forever and ever.

EXODUS 15:18

Sunday

John the Baptist Prepares the Way

LUKE 3:1-23

Before an important person goes to visit a place, some of that person's employees go first. They prepare for the arrival of the important person. They get everything ready.

That is what John the Baptist did. He got everyone ready for Jesus. John preached about Jesus, the Son of God, who would save them from their sins. John lived in the wilderness and ate locusts and dressed in camel's hair clothes. He told everyone to "Get ready because the Lord is coming!" John even baptized Jesus when he began his ministry.

What was John's job? How would you feel if you were the one to baptize Jesus?

Dear God,
John's job was important.
Someone had to tell the people to
watch for Jesus. I can tell people
about Jesus too. Amen.

Prepare the way for the Lord, make his paths straight!

LUKE 3:4

Peter Learns a Lesson

ACTS 10

One thing about Peter is that you always knew what he was thinking. He was not the strong, silent type. Peter was very firm about things like eating food that had been sacrificed to false gods; and talking to certain kinds of people about God.

Then one night Peter had a dream. He dreamed he was hungry and a sheet came down from heaven full of food. But it was all food that he didn't think he should eat, and he said it was unclean. God said to him, "If God makes something clean, don't call it unclean!"

From that time on Peter knew that he should tell every-one about God's love, not just people he thought were acceptable.

Are there people you do not like? Why?

Are there people God does not like?

Dear God,
You want everyone to hear about you. Don't let me keep quiet about your love because I have decided someone shouldn't hear. Let me tell everyone I meet.
Amen.

God doesn't play favorites. Rather, whoever respects God and does what is right is acceptable to him in any nation.

ACTS 10:34-35

Paul Keeps on Serving

ACTS 21:1-14

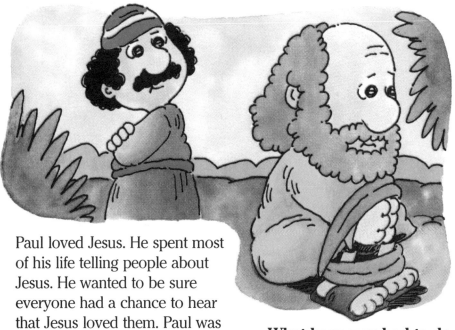

Paul loved Jesus. He spent most of his life telling people about Jesus. He wanted to be sure everyone had a chance to hear that Jesus loved them. Paul was planning to go to Jerusalem to talk about Jesus some more.

A man named Agabus came to Paul. He could tell the future. He took off Paul's belt and tied his hands and feet. He warned Paul that if he went to Jerusalem, that's how he would be treated. All of Paul's friends tried to stop him from going.

Paul said he wasn't afraid. He would go to Jerusalem no matter what. He was even ready to die for the sake of the Lord.

What have you had to do that was hard?

When have you been afraid?

Dear God,
Thank you for Paul's example of serving you. Help me to have courage like Paul had.
Amen.

Don't let anyone move you off the foundation of your faith. Always excel in the work you do for the Lord.

1 CORINTHIANS 15:58

Jesus Chooses His Family

LUKE 6:12-16

Jesus had many friends and followers. One day he went up on a mountainside to pray. After he prayed he called his followers to come to him. Then he chose twelve of them to be his special friends. They would be as close as family to him. Jesus spent many hours teaching these twelve and preparing them to carry on his work. The twelve were called apostles. Jesus wanted them to travel around from town to town telling about him. He even gave them special abilities, like being able to heal and raise people from the dead.

Who are your close friends?

How can you tell about Jesus like the apostles?

Dear God,
The apostles had to leave their homes and families to follow Jesus. That must have been hard. Thank you that they kept sharing the good news of Jesus. Amen.

I don't call you servants anymore, because a servant doesn't know what his master is doing. But I have called you friends because I have made known to you everything that I have heard from my Father. JOHN 15:15

Thursday

John, Jesus' Friend

MATTHEW 17:1; JOHN 13:23; 19:26; REV. 1:9

Week 48

John was called the disciple whom Jesus loved. He traveled with Jesus and saw many of the miracles that Jesus did. Jesus took John along with Peter up on a mountain where Jesus was changed right in front of them and Moses and Elijah came and talked with him.

John was also there when Jesus was crucified. Jesus looked down from the cross and saw him standing there. He asked John to take care of his mother, Mary.

God gave John a glimpse of what the future holds. John wrote that vision down in the book of Revelation.

What was John called?
How can you tell that John was special to Jesus?

Dear God,
I'm glad to be special to you. I'm glad Jesus had special friends because then you understand how I feel about my friends. Amen.

Be devoted to each other like a loving family. Excel in showing respect for each other. ROMANS 12:10

351

Friday

Timothy, the Young Preacher

1 TIMOTHY 4:11; 2 TIMOTHY

Paul called Timothy his son. That may be because Paul spent so much time with Timothy teaching him about God and how to work with churches. Paul even sent Timothy to some of the churches he had started to see how they were doing.

Paul wrote two letters to Timothy. They are now 1 and 2 Timothy in our Bible. The second letter was helpful in teaching Timothy to not be afraid. Paul told him to never be ashamed of the Gospel he was preaching. He said Timothy was definitely going to face hard times ahead, but Paul said, "Be strong," because God would give him strength to get through anything.

Did Paul say Timothy could expect an easy life?
Where would Timothy's strength come from?

Dear God,
I'm glad that Paul said Timothy could work for God even though he was young. I want to work for you and I'm young too. Amen.

My child, find your source of strength in the kindness of Christ Jesus.

2 TIMOTHY 2:1

Jamie's Favorite

"Mom, know what story I like to hear?" Jamie asked.

"No, what story?" Mom said as she sat down next to Jamie.

"I like how the apostle Paul told Timothy that he could serve God even though he was young. Timothy could even be an example to older people."

"I agree that is a neat thing. So, can you think of ways that you can be an example to people?"

"Well, I can always be friendly. I can pray and read my Bible so I stay close to God. And I can tell my friends how God loves them," Jamie listed a few ideas.

What are some other ways you can be an example to people?

Do you try to serve God, even though you are young?

Dear God,
I'm sure there are ways I can serve you that I haven't even thought of. Show me what they are. Thank you that even children are important to you. Amen.

Never be ashamed to tell others about our Lord.

2 TIMOTHY 1:8

Children in the Bible

Samuel Hears Voices

1 SAMUEL 3

Samuel's mother had prayed for a long time for a baby. She even promised God that if he gave her a baby, she would give the child back to God to serve him. So now Samuel lived in the temple with the priest, Eli.

One night Samuel was almost asleep when he heard someone call his name. He ran to see what Eli wanted. But it was not Eli who had called him. This happened three times. Finally Eli realized that it must be God calling Samuel. It was! He had a special message to give Samuel.

How would you feel about living away from your parents?

Would you be afraid if you heard God call your name?

Dear God,
Help me to know what you want me to do. Amen.

God didn't give us a cowardly spirit but a spirit of power, love, and good judgment. 2 TIMOTHY 1:7

354

A Slave Girl

2 KINGS 5:1-14

Naaman was an officer in the army. He was a great soldier and his commander liked him very much. But the sad thing was that Naaman had a terrible skin disease called leprosy. Lepers could not live around other people because the disease was so contagious.

Naaman's wife had a young slave girl who had been captured from Israel. She was sad to hear that Naaman had leprosy. The girl told Naaman's wife that he should go see the prophet Elisha. She was certain the prophet could heal Naaman.

Naaman's wife told him what the girl said. He went to see Elisha and was healed of the leprosy.

How did this child help another person?

How could you help another person?

Dear God,
The little slave girl knew the answer to Naaman's problem and she wasn't too shy to tell someone. Thank you for showing me that a child can help with a grown-up's problem. Amen.

Even a child makes himself known by his actions, whether his deeds are pure or right.   PROVERBS 20:11

355

Josiah

2 KINGS 22:1—23:3

Josiah was only eight years old when he became king of Judah. Josiah wanted to live for God and his role model was King David. Josiah knew that the temple of God had not been used for a long time. So he hired some men to fix it up. While they were working, they found a book with God's laws written in it.

When the young king read the laws, he was upset that the people had not been following them. So he called all the people together and read the laws to them. He threw all the idols out of the temple and told the people to follow God's rules. He punished any who still wanted to worship idols. A young boy led the people back to God.

Would you want to be an eight-year-old king?

How do you think Josiah handled the responsibility?

Dear God,
I want to follow your rules too.
Please help me be brave enough
to follow you. Thank you for
helping me. Amen.

Even when I am afraid, I still trust you. PSALM 56:3

Children Who Wanted to See Jesus

LUKE 18:15-17

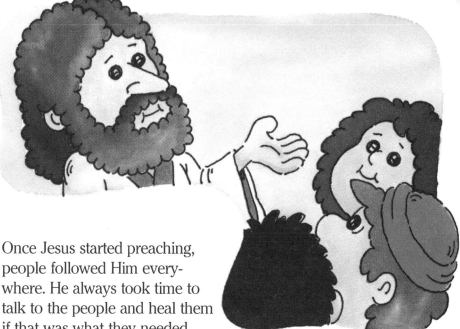

Once Jesus started preaching, people followed Him everywhere. He always took time to talk to the people and heal them if that was what they needed.

One day some mothers brought their young children to see Jesus. They hoped that Jesus would bless their babies.

But Jesus' followers stopped the mothers from getting close to him. They said, "Jesus is too busy teaching the grown-ups. He doesn't have time for children."

Jesus heard them, and he said, "Don't stop the children from coming to me. Any grown-ups who want to come to God, must trust like a child does."

Which grown-ups talk to you?

Does Jesus only care about grown-ups?

Dear God,
Thank you that Jesus took time for the children. I am glad that children are important to you. I am glad that I am important to you. Amen.

Jesus said, "Don't stop the children from coming to me!"

LUKE 18:16

357

The Boy with a Lunch

JOHN 6:1-15

Jesus had been teaching all day. He was tired, but people kept coming so he kept teaching. Finally it was time for the people to eat. Jesus asked, "Where are we going to get food for all these people?"

Philip said, "It would take over half a year's pay to buy food for all these people." But another disciple spoke up. He said, "There is a young boy here who has a lunch of five loaves of bread and two fish. That's all the food we can find."

The boy was happy to give his lunch to Jesus. Jesus blessed the food and broke it into pieces. Over five thousand people had food to eat. And there was food left over.

Would you have given your lunch to Jesus?

How do you think the boy felt when all those people ate from his lunch?

Dear God,
That boy must have been excited to have Jesus use his lunch. I would do whatever I could to help Jesus. Amen.

I am the bread of life   JOHN 6:48

Paul's Nephew

ACTS 23:12-22

Paul was in prison because he kept preaching about God. That made some of the church leaders angry. Some of them promised each other that they would not eat or drink until Paul was dead. But Paul's nephew heard about their plan and he hurried to tell Paul.

Paul sent him to tell one of the commanders. When the commander heard what the plan was, he got some guards and they sneaked Paul out of the prison in the middle of the night. The boy saved Paul's life!

Why was Paul in prison? How can you tell that the boy loved his Uncle Paul?

Dear God,
Wow! A boy saved the life of the great apostle Paul. I pray that someday you will be able to use me to do something important.
Amen.

Encourage each other and strengthen one another as you are doing.

1 THESSALONIANS 5:11

How Can I Serve?

Jamie was sitting on the couch staring at nothing when Mom came into the room. "What's the matter? You look like you lost your best friend," Mom said.

"Oh, I was just thinking about the stories we've read about how kids did things for God. I haven't ever done anything great for him. Sometimes I'm not even sure he hears my prayers," Jamie whispered.

"Everybody feels that way sometimes," Mom said. "But if you want to do things for God and you keep close to him by reading the Bible and praying, then I'm sure you will someday."

Mom always knew the right thing to say.

Have you ever felt like God didn't have anything for you to do?

How often do you talk to God and read his Word?

Dear God,
I know I'm just a kid and my whole life is ahead of me, but I want to do things for you now. Please show me ways I can serve you. Amen.

Always be ready to defend the hope you have when anyone asks you to explain it.

1 PETER 3:15

Getting Along with Others

Sunday

Love Each Other

1 JOHN 3:18; 4:7-8

The main message that Jesus taught about getting along with each other is that we should love each other. We should love each other because love comes from God. He loved each of us so completely that he sent his Son to die for our sins.

That kind of love is our example. So if we do not love each other, then it shows that we are not truly a part of God's family. Our love for each other will not just be with words, either. We will do whatever we can to help each other. A good way to check if God is controlling our lives is to see if we are loving other people.

How much does God love you?

What is one way you can show God's love to others?

Dear God,
It isn't always easy to love the people around me. Some of them are not very lovable. Love them through me. I want everyone to know that I love you. Amen.

God is love.

1 JOHN 4:16

361

Monday

Encouraging Each Other

ROMANS 12:18; 14:19; 15:2; EPHESIANS 4:12

How do you feel when you are around someone who tells you how good you are doing, or how nice you look, or what a kind person you are? It makes you feel good about yourself, doesn't it?

That is one of the things we are supposed to do for each other. We should look for good things to say to others that will encourage them. Be careful not to say unkind things to others. When we are encouraging each other, we can all work together better to spread the message of God's love.

How do others usually encourage you?

What could you say to encourage a friend?

Dear God,
It feels so good to hear kind things said about me. I know everyone likes to hear nice things. Help me remember to say kind and encouraging things to others. Amen.

We should all be concerned about our neighbor and the good things that will build his faith.

ROMANS 15:2

362

Working Together

ECCLESIASTES 4:9-10; 1 CORINTHIANS 9:19-23;

When you are sad, do you want your friends to ignore you? Of course not, you want them to sit down and listen to how you are feeling. If you need help to be strong or brave, you want your friend to help you.

One of the best parts of having a friend is sharing the good times and the bad times. If your friend is only with you in the good times, but disappears during the hard times, he is not a real friend. The Bible tells us to help each other and be there to strengthen our friends.

When have you needed a friend?

When was a time that you strengthened a friend?

Dear God,
Friends make life a lot easier.
Help me be a friend that shows
God's love. Amen.

Two people are better than one because together they have a good reward for their hard work. If one falls, the other can help his friend get up.

ECCLESIASTES 4:9-10

363

Forgive Each Other

MATTHEW 18:21-22; EPHESIANS 4:32; 3:13

When you are angry with someone, do you keep thinking about what they have done? Do you let yourself get more and more angry?

That is not what the Bible says to do. The Bible says when someone does something to you that hurts you or makes you angry, forgive them. There is no limit to how many times you should forgive. You should forgive others, just as God, in Christ, forgave you.

When you forgive others, you will feel good, and they will be happy. Then you can work together to share the good news.

When were you forgiven for something?

Is there someone you should forgive now?

Dear God,
Sometimes forgiving is not easy.
Help me forgive others as many
times as it takes for us to be
friends. Help me to show your
love by forgiving others. Amen.

If you forgive the failures of others, your heavenly Father will also forgive you.

MATTHEW 6:14

Thursday

Keep Meeting Together

ACTS 2:42; HEBREWS 10:25

Do you enjoy going to church? Are the members of your church like family to you? We should never get tired of meeting together with the people who believe the same things we do. Meeting together with our church members will help us become close to them.

Meeting together gives us chances to encourage each other. We can also help each other stay close to God and true in our understanding of the Bible.

Who are your church friends?
When have those friends helped you?

Dear God,
Thank you for my church. Help me to be an important part of it. Amen.

Comfort each other!
1 THESSALONIANS 4:18

365

Be Unified

JEREMIAH 32:39; JOHN 17:21; ACTS 2:42

What would happen if one of your legs wanted to go one way and the other one wanted to go a different way? That wouldn't work, would it? It doesn't work with the body of Christ, either. When we work together with other believers we can do great things for God. But we must be unified. That means we have the same goals and we can work together to spread the Good News of God's love.

Jesus wanted us to work together the way he and his Father work together. Sometimes we might even have to change our plans so we can work better with other people.

Have you ever been part of a team?

When have you had to give up your plans to keep peace?

Dear God,
Help me be flexible. Help me to work together with other people in order to spread your Word.
Amen.

I am in them, and you are in me, so that they are completely united. In this way the world knows that you have sent me and that you have loved them just as you loved me.   JOHN 17:23

Jamie Is Encouraged

"Jesus loves me, this I know," Jamie sang at the top of his lungs. When song time was over Mrs. Brown came over to him.

"Jamie, you are one of the best singers I have ever had in this Sunday School class," she said.

Jamie looked at her shyly. "I don't think I stay on the tune real good," he said quietly.

"Well, I like how you sing with so much energy. It sounds like you really mean what you are singing."

How do you think Jamie sang after that?

What could you encourage someone about?

Dear God,
I want to be an encourager. Help me see the good in others and tell them about it. Amen.

We love because God loved us first.

1 JOHN 4:19

The Book of James

True Religion Does Not Come Easy

JAMES 1:2-15

Everyone has problems. Every person is tempted to do wrong things. But, when you face hard times, be happy! Going through hard experiences will help your faith in God grow stronger. As your faith gets stronger, you are learning to live more like Jesus.

God will help you know the right choices to make, if you ask him and really believe that he will answer you. So when life gets tough, keep on going. And remember that God will give you chances to let your faith grow, but he will not tempt you to do wrong things. So when you are tempted, always say NO!

What problems do you have?

When have you been tempted to do wrong?

Dear God,
Thank you for problems that help me learn to trust in you. Give me strength to say no when temptation comes along. Amen.

When you are tested in many different ways, you should be very happy.

JAMES 1:2

Faith Starts Everything

JAMES 1:16-27

When someone gives you a gift, what do you do with it? Put it on the floor without opening it? No, you probably rip the paper off, eager to see what is inside.

Salvation is a gift that needs to be opened. We can hear all about how God loves us and Jesus died and rose again for us. But if we do not accept his salvation, it is like a gift that is never opened.

When we accept God's salvation, we are changed. We start doing what the Bible says to do. That is one way to see that our hearts are turned toward God.

When did you open the gift of salvation?

Who can you share that gift with?

Dear God,
Thank you for the gift of salvation. It is too good to keep to myself. Help me share it with everyone. Amen.

Do what God's word says. Don't merely listen to it, or you will fool yourselves.   JAMES 1:22

369

Live Your Faith

JAMES 2:1–2:26

"Do unto others as you would have them do unto you." Some people talk about how much they love God. They talk about what wonderful Christians they are. But, they do not do anything that shows that they love God.

Just doing good things will not get you into heaven. But if you do love God, it will show in how you live. Faith that comes out in your life does not play favorites. You will love all people and want to share God's love with all people.

Just believing who God is, without accepting the gift of salvation is not good enough. People who do that will not be in heaven.

How do you want others to treat you?

How do you show love to others?

Dear God,
Help me to live my faith. My life may be the only Bible some people ever see. Amen.

Love your neighbor as yourself.

JAMES 2:8

Wisdom Comes from God

JAMES 3:1-18

Big ships that sail across the ocean are guided by a small piece of metal called a rudder. The rudder being turned one way or the other changes the direction of the ship.

The rudder of our bodies is the tongue. Friends are made or lost by what we say. Wars are started because of words.

Knowing the right things to say takes wisdom. A wise person is peaceful and kind, not selfish or greedy. He doesn't show favoritism. Wisdom shows what God is like. This wisdom is a gift of God. He will give you wisdom, if you ask him.

When have you said something hurtful to a friend?
How did you feel afterward?

Dear God,
Help me show wisdom by how I speak to others. Give me a kind and loving heart. And let it show in my words. Amen.

However, the wisdom that comes from above is first of all pure. Then it is peace-loving, gentle, willing to obey, filled with mercy and good works, impartial, and sincere.

JAMES 3:17

Thursday

Demonstrate Your Faith

JAMES 4:1-17

Do you enjoy playing with a friend who is selfish and will not share his toys? How do you feel about that person? Most fights and arguments happen because one person is thinking only of himself.

You can have anything you want by asking God, you don't have to fight with someone else to get it. But, when you ask God, it must be with the right motives, not just for your own pleasure.

Don't say bad things about other people. You have no right to judge other people. That is breaking God's law. And don't brag about what you are going to do tomorrow. Just say that you will do whatever God wants you to do.

When have you been selfish?
Did your selfishness end up in a fight with a friend?

Dear God,
Help me to show your love by how I treat my friends. Help me to not argue and say bad things about them. Amen.

Place yourselves under God's authority.

JAMES 4:7

Show Your Faith by Prayer

JAMES 5:13-20

Do you ever wonder if God hears your prayers? Does he do what you ask him to do?

The answer is yes. God does hear your prayers. In fact, when James says to pray in faith, that means really believing God can do what you ask. That kind of prayer can even make a sick person well.

A good person who truly loves God and wants to serve him will have powerful prayers. Anyone can have powerful prayers. Just believe that God hears you and will answer you, and then your prayers will be very effective.

What have you earnestly prayed for?

What answers has God given you?

Dear God,
Prayer can change the world. I really believe that. Thank you for hearing and answering my prayers. Amen.

Prayers offered by people who have God's approval are powerful.

JAMES 5:16

Saturday

Jamie's Faith

"You make me so mad. I'm not gonna be your friend anymore!" Jamie shouted. Tommy ran across the yard to his own house, eager to get away from Jamie's anger.

"What's going on?" Mom asked.

"I'm so mad at Tommy. We always have to play what he wants," Jamie was still shouting.

"Jamie, do you think you are showing Tommy God's love by how you are acting? It sounds like you are being selfish and saying mean things."

"But, Tommy . . ." Jamie began.

"You are responsible only for you, not for what Tommy does," Mom interrupted.

How do you think Jamie felt after Mom's talk?

Did Tommy see God's love in Jamie?

Dear God,
It's hard to remember that every day, in everything I do, I should show your love. Help me do that. Amen.

Are any of you wise and insightful? Show this by living the right way, by having humility that comes from wisdom.

JAMES 3:13

374

Sunday

Jesus Is Coming

LUKE 17:29-36

Jesus told his followers that someday he would come back and take his children to heaven. We will stay there with him forever. But, we must be ready to go with him anytime. There will be no warning when he comes back. Just like in the days of Noah when the flood came and surprised all the people, Jesus will return suddenly.

We should be busy telling everyone about Jesus because when he comes there will not be time to decide to follow him. Two people will be in a bed, one will go with him and the other will be left. Two women will be working in a field; one will be taken and the other left.

Are you ready to go with Jesus at anytime?

Who do you need to tell about him?

Dear God,
My friends and family need to know you. I want us all to be in heaven together someday. Let me tell them soon. Amen.

If you add these qualities to your faith you will also add the wealth of entering into the eternal kingdom of our Lord and Savior Jesus Christ.

2 PETER 1:11

375

Judgment

1 CORINTHIANS 3:12-15, 4:5

The day is coming when every person will answer for the life he has lived. If you have lived wisely, showing God's love and telling others about him, then you do not need to be afraid of judgment. If you have lived selfishly, not caring at all how God says you should live, then you will not be allowed into God's heaven.

When that judgment day comes, God will know everything about you. Even the things that are secrets in your heart. Everything that is hidden will be made known on that day.

Are there things you have done that no one knows about?

How does it feel to know that God knows all your secrets?

Dear God,
Please forgive the secrets in my heart. I'm sorry for those things. Thank you for loving me. Amen.

Your heavenly master will reward all of us for whatever good we do.

EPHESIANS 6:8

Believer's Hope

ROMANS 8:38-39; COLOSSIANS 1:5; 1 JOHN 2:28

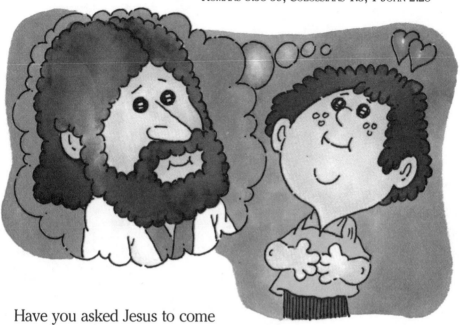

Have you asked Jesus to come into your heart? Do you believe that he died for your sins and that he came back to life? Did you know he lives in heaven and will someday come to take you there, along with everyone else who believes in him?

Jesus promised to come and get his children some day. And he never breaks a promise. So we know that whatever happens to us in life will not change that. We know that someday we will be with him, and with everyone we love who is part of God's family.

When have you broken a promise?

Are you glad that Jesus does not break promises?

Dear God,
I'm going to be in heaven someday. That is great! Thank you for always keeping your promises. Thank you that I can look forward to this one. Amen.

Now, dear children, live in Christ so that when he appears we will have confidence. Then we won't turn from him in shame when he comes.

1 JOHN 2:28

Signs of His Return

MATTHEW 24:3-14

Just before Jesus comes back, the world will be very confusing. Some people may go around saying they are Jesus, but of course, they are not. There will be wars and rumors of wars across the world.

The world will not be a happy place for believers. That's because many people will not want to hear about Jesus' love. But, just when you think you can't take anymore, Jesus will come like a light in the sky. He will take his children to heaven.

Are you looking forward to Jesus' return? Are you ready?

Dear God,
Sometimes I wish Jesus would come today because I want to be with him. But, I still know people who wouldn't come to heaven, so help me tell them, now! Amen.

Then the sign of the Son of Man will appear in the sky. All the people on earth will cry in agony when they see the Son of Man coming on the clouds in the sky with power and great glory.

MATTHEW 24:30

Heavenly Treasures

MATTHEW 6:19-24

Jesus said we should not get caught up in making money and being rich here on earth. We should concentrate on what is really important. That is living for him and telling others about him. When we do those things we are putting our treasures in heaven. No thief can steal the treasures we put in heaven; they are safe forever.

There is nothing wrong with making money, but it should never be more important than doing God's work. Find happiness in God, not in things.

How do you put treasures in heaven?

Do you always want more and more things?

Dear God,
Help me keep things straight so I put my treasures in heaven.
Amen.

You cannot serve God and wealth.

MATTHEW 6:24

Praising God Forever

REVELATION 7:12; 19

When we get to heaven we will be there forever. What will we do all the time? We will praise God for everything he has ever done. Praise him for his great power that made the world! Praise him that he won over evil. Praise God because he rules forever. Praise God because he loves us.

Everything God does is great and wonderful, his ways are always right. God is holy!

What can you praise God for right now?

Thank him for all he has done for you.

Dear God,
Forever won't be long enough to praise you. Thank you for everything you have done and will do. Amen.

The kingdom of the world has become the kingdom of our Lord and of his Christ, and he will rule as king forever and ever

REVELATION 11:15

Hurry Up!

Is there someone you need to pray for?
Who should you tell about God?

"Mom, if Jesus is coming back soon we have to hurry up and tell everyone about him. Some of my friends still don't believe in him. They won't have the chance to decide when he comes. They have to decide now," Jamie cried.

"You're right, Jamie. We should be telling everyone we know. And, we should be praying for them. We want everyone we love to be with us in heaven!"

Dear God,
I want all my family to be with me in heaven. Help me tell them about you and help them listen. Amen.

Honor, majesty, power, and authority before time began, now, and for eternity belong to the only God, our Savior, through Jesus Christ our Lord. Amen.

JUDE 25

381

—